NOTES ON POLITICAL ECONOMY

NOTES

ON

POLITICAL ECONOMY

AS APPLICABLE TO

THE UNITED STATES

BY

A SOUTHERN PLANTER

[Nathaniel A. Ware]

[1844]

REPRINTS OF ECONOMIC CLASSICS

AUGUSTUS M. KELLEY · PUBLISHERS
NEW YORK · 1967

First Edition 1844

(New York: Leavitt, Trow & Co., 1844)

Reprinted 1967 by
AUGUSTUS M. KELLEY PUBLISHERS

Library of Congress Catalogue Card Number
66-19698

PRINTED IN THE UNITED STATES OF AMERICA
by SENTRY PRESS, NEW YORK, N. Y. 10019

NOTES

ON

POLITICAL ECONOMY,

AS APPLICABLE TO

THE UNITED STATES.

BY

A SOUTHERN PLANTER.

NEW-YORK:

LEAVITT, TROW, AND CO.

1844.

PREFACE.

THESE Notes on Political Economy, as applicable to the United States, were written within the last two years, partly to give expression to thoughts that occurred to the author, and partly to occupy and amuse his leisure moments. Friends advised their publication, and they are now given, for what they are worth, to the public. The author hopes that they may be read with care, and without prejudice, their suggestions improved upon, and that they may lead to some good results. The whole United States will find their attention directed, both in principle and detail, to a subject that embraces all interests; and the Southern States particularly, with which the author stands identified, by birth and interest, are requested to read these Notes in reference to their staple productions, wants, and operations. Whatever defects may be found in the work, the author hopes to get credit for good intentions.

CONTENTS.

CHAPTER XXXI.

CHAPTER XXXII.

CHAPTER XXXIII.

NOTES ON POLITICAL ECONOMY.

CHAPTER I.

DEFINITION.

POLITICAL ECONOMY is a science that embraces
and regards all measures calculated to advance the
prosperity of a nation. This is its positive and
direct object; but, negatively, it questions all such
measures and policies as are thought injurious to a
country's interest, or that from their nature seem
calculated to retard or interfere with its prosperity.

This science is in its nature essentially practical, and should be treated in a plain, practical
way. Adam Smith, Mr. Say, and others who wrote
upon this subject, were too abstract and theoreti-
cal for common use. They either presupposed
facts and circumstances to fit their theories, or left
it to the imagination of their readers to shape
them. It became harder to find the cases to which
they apply, than to mark the theories and princi-

ples that are applicable to such cases, or to trace
the results that flowed from them.   Political economy should be treated in a manner so plain that
all can understand it; that a child may run and
read its practical uses and natural results.   Plain
working men have to do with its operations, and
they are the sort that prove its principles, and
make the best and most available suggestions to
the legislators of the countries to which they appertain.   This class of persons are in possession of
the facts, and acquainted with the circumstances
that form the basis of all valuable operations.   It
would be " the cart before the horse," in regard to
such men, to begin with theories.   They must first
have the facts, be in possession of all circumstances
of the country, its markets, its wants, its labor, its
capacity, its capital, and materials, and then it is
easy to combine them and show the effects of any
policy or operation.   Theories and results flow from
such a practical combination, and are its legitimate
and natural offspring.

Many of the rules and maxims of these standard writers are doubtless true and valuable when
the case fits them.   They would be much more
striking and conclusive, however, if worked out by
practice, in connection with a suitable set of facts
and circumstances, than when read from books, in
the dark abstract way in which they treat them
and state them.   All the doctrine of wages, labor,
capital, profits, monopolies, and so forth, that fill

up their volumes to such an extent, is true only in reference to circumstances, and the results are the one thing or the other, good or bad, useful or injurious, accordingly as these circumstances exist or change. I shall therefore treat this subject strictly and literally in relation to the circumstances of these United States, and make all my suggestions and base all my policies upon that safe and natural foundation. Measures that thus rest upon facts, and look to the circumstances of the country, must be right—cannot err. The case becomes then made up, and the consequences aimed at flow certainly and naturally therefrom. Fortunately for mankind, and for nations, the facts present themselves in a way to be seen by all that are desirous of seeking truth or benefiting their country, and can be cited and stated so as to convince the whole mass of the people.

CHAPTER II.

' GOVERNED BY CIRCUMSTANCES,' IS THE GOLDEN RULE IN POLITICAL ECONOMY.

I WOULD lay down this rule or maxim as the only available one in this science. The political economist, and the governors or legislators that would wish to place their country upon the proper ground, and promote its prosperity, must regard it or fail. In all modifications of the tariff; in all propositions to promote agriculture, commerce, or manufactures; in all laws or arrangements that go to affect labor, or change the order of things, the only question should be, Do the circumstances of the country favor it; or, do the interests of the nation require it? is a case made out to fit or call for the measure in question? and what is the real condition of things in reference to the proposition? not what did Adam Smith or Mr. Say write or lay down?

That mighty difference between national wealth and greatness, and national poverty and wretchedness, is, nine times in ten, brought about by totally disregarding the circumstances of countries in the latter case, and turning them to account and obeying them in the former. Servilely copying the example of other countries, whether their circumstances be similar to ours or not, never fails to mislead and produce confusion. We may easily trace all the national degradation and misery that history sets forth to misrule, or gross neglect of the circumstances that they were surrounded with, and should have consulted. I will here state some cases, both real and hypothetical, where circumstances should or did govern, and give the proper direction to the industry and labor of man, and of nations, and lead to wealth and comfort.

1st. In the realities of history. Venice and Genoa could not have failed to push commerce and the carrying trade for all Europe. They had the ships; were in a confined or insular situation; and emboldened by free institutions to undertake what lay before them and promised so much profit and consideration. The Crusades threw all Europe upon them, and unsealed the trade of the East to their enterprise.

Mexico and Peru could not have failed to work the mines that lay around them, and pour forth the precious metals to the whole earth. These gave the means of procuring food and clothes from abroad, and even luxuries to any extent.

These United States, for twenty-five years after their revolution, with a fertile soil, few laborers, and a good market in Europe for their provisions, did right in pushing agriculture, and their shipping interest. Europe, engaged in long wars, had need of their provisions to feed their armies, and of their tonnage to neutralize their commerce. Many other cases might be adduced from history, to show that circumstances did govern, and give to labor the proper direction.

2d. Hypothetically. A country, naturally sterile in its soil, but underlaid with the richest mines of the precious and useful metals, ought to, and would, as a matter of course, work these mines, even if she had to buy her provisions and clothing from abroad. She could well afford to do this, because she would have the means of paying for them, and her labor would evidently be employed to the best advantage.

A young nation inhabiting a rich and fertile country, with but few laborers, and a good and constant market for corn and other provisions, would of course pursue agriculture, and enrich herself by its productions. They could by their surplus purchase clothes and even luxuries, and have prosperity.

An isolated people with but little territory, and surrounded by fish and pearls, would, as a matter of course, cast their nets and push commerce and navigation. Under such circumstances many small communities have become wealthy and important, and even luxurious.

A tropical population with fertile soil, and unlimited markets for sugar, cotton, coffee, cocoa, and other tropical productions, would naturally cultivate those staples, and grow rich and luxurious.

In all these real and supposititious cases, and many others that might be enumerated, labor could not or did not fail to take the most profitable channels. The circumstances in which they were placed naturally pointed to these results. In all such cases we might mark the controlling influence of the above rule, that circumstances do govern and should direct the course of labor. In the cases of this sort there was or could be no occasion for the action of the Government to direct industry, nor any theories of the political economist necessary to develope their resources. I shall in the next chapter enumerate some cases that would require legislation, and even protection and bounties, to put labor in the most productive channels.

CHAPTER III.

CASES REQUIRING PROTECTION, BOUNTY, OR SOME ACT OF THE GOVERNMENT.

WHEN a nation has a part of its population idle, or from immigration and growth acquires surplus labor, such surplus labor ought to be induced to become productive. If all the usual occupations be pre-engaged and full, then such surplus labor should be turned to some new employment, or into some new channel of industry, and made to produce some new staples, or develope some new products in agriculture, or some new articles of manufacture that would be available. Should it be necessary, protection and bounties should be extended by the government. It becomes a leading policy in all governments, to prevent any portion of its population being idle, and becoming not only clogs upon the community, but vicious.

Whenever the usual markets of a people become overloaded, either by the demand diminishing, or the production increasing, a portion of the labor should be drawn off, and by proper protection or rewards induced into other and more profitable channels of business. This not only gives new resources, but relieves the business already overcharged.

Whenever markets open for certain articles or productions promising greater profit than the usual occupations, a stimulus should be imparted by the government, to supply such better or more profitable markets.

Whenever new resources of mines or products be discovered of a nature manifestly profitable, they should be developed, and a portion of the labor of the country less profitably engaged turned into them by proper rewards and protection.

When the independence of a nation, and the comfort of the people require certain things to be produced, such as iron, copper, lead, coal, blankets, flannels, and any such articles of first necessity, they should be protected, and their production made certain by the proper bounties and inducements. Woe betide the nation that depends on foreign countries, perhaps enemies, for such things! It is a primary policy, or should be, in nations, to have such things produced up to the consumption or wants of the people.

In all such cases as the above cited, and many others that do annually occur in the history of nations, it may be necessary to have the aid of the government to bring about the changes in labor that circumstances so plainly call for, and that even where greater profits might accrue. Protections and bounties may be required to break up the usual channels of labor, and give to it a new direction. Circumstances govern these sort of cases just as strongly as those where labor takes a voluntary direction. The change of habit, the preparation necessary, the loss of time in acquiring skill, and scarcity of capital, lie in the way of individual enterprise, and prevent any movement or investment in the new channel without such inducements or guaranty.

CHAPTER IV.

PROTECTION.

In the last named cases we have stated that protection, and even bounties, might be necessary to give new directions to labor and capital. The policy of protection is too manifest in many cases to be questioned by any political economist, and the practice has prevailed more or less in all ages and in all nations. Taunt me not, then, with the quaint argument that " the let-alone system is the best." Tell me not that, under all circumstances, individuals will not only find out the most profitable lines of industry and business, but execute them, and realize the profits incident thereto! that no action of the government is necessary in any case, no protection or bounty required! I answer, yes, and appeal to experience to support me. A young nation never has much capital, not enough to put to hazard, or in any manner jeopardize. Scarcely any new line of business can be entered upon successfully without capital and skill. No new mine could be extensively wrought, no new culture requiring expensive machinery, such as sugar, could be instituted, nor any of those manufactories started where much machinery is necessary.

There is always a loss of time, and generally a failure of profit sustained by persons commencing new business. This is the tax ignorance pays for skill and experience, and from such considerations alone, individuals are deterred from new business requiring such skill and capital. In order to compensate for this delay necessary to the acquiring of the skill, and for the delay also in removing capital from one business to another, and the time lost in the preparation, as well as the almost certain failure of profits at the start, is the protection or bounty called for and given. This protection or bounty, even should it amount to a tax on the consumers, is only temporary; because, when it shall have induced the capital and skill necessary, and built up a competition, the consumers and the whole country are more than compensated by the greater cheapness and better quality of the articles thus produced. This I will be prepared to prove in a subsequent chapter, by the proper catalogues of things thus produced in the United States, and their prices before and after protection. I will here merely say that every production, the result of protection, in this country, has been brought cheaper and better into the market than before such protection.

A brief account of the United States, and the productions of her labor, will show how much protection has already accomplished, and the necessity of giving much more extension to the principle. For twenty-five years after our revolution the labor of this country took the proper direction without any protection. It was taken up in agriculture and commerce. Provisions were needed in Europe to sustain the long wars waged, and tonnage to neutralize and render safe their commerce; thus originating the carrying trade. As soon as Europe could dispense with our provisions and tonnage she did, and our market for agricultural products became limited and much diminished, and the carrying trade was completely cut up. The production of staples, such as tobacco, rice, and cotton, increasing, owing to the wants of the European powers, gave some continued employment to our laborers, and for a time were profitable. That profit, however, became a curse to the country, by filling it with slaves, to the exclusion of free labor, and leaving the northern and free states almost in distress for the want of productive labor.

In this state of labor, without the skill or capital, or any special protection for manufacturing, a portion of laborers turned into the handicraft occupations, because no capital and but little skill were necessary to commence in them. Hence shoes, boots, hats, cabinet and household furniture, carriages, tailoring, carving, gilding, painting, chemicals, plantation cutlery, paper, glass, leather, all things of leather, fur, and wood, and a thousand other things, requiring little or no capital or machinery except the hands, were entered upon and made of good quality and taste up to the consumption of the country. All the above articles were made without tariff protection and with success, because no capital, or expensive machinery, or delay, was necessary to their operations—nothing but a few cheap tools and the fingers.

In the handicraft operations there is no dividend to be made to capital. It is all the creation of labor; and let the profits be much or little, and the articles sell for a high or low price, yet it all redounded to the fabricator, and gave him a certainty of support, which encouraged him to go ahead. The above facts in regard to our success in the handicraft occupations prove volumes to our political economists. They prove our success in this country, where we are told there is no surplus labor, and that if there were spare laborers, they need not hope to compete with Europe, where wages are so low, without the very best sort of labor-saving machinery; that it must be by such aids, not by naked labor, that we may hope to equalize or approximate the labor of Europe. Our success not only proves our skill and ingenuity, but that we have surplus labor in this country.

All of our manufacturing operations were confined to the handicraft, until the embargo, the non-intercourse, and the last war with England, cut off our trade and supply from abroad. Then dire necessity operated upon us, and the double or treble value of all goods made by machinery, aided by high protecting duties laid on by the Congress of the United States, induced capitalists and skill to commence the manufacturing of cotton, woollen, iron, sugar, salt, and many other things of great necessity. During those times of difficulty much skill was acquired and much capital invested in those branches requiring machinery, and our progress and success were great for the time.   As soon as these difficulties ceased, and peace and commerce resumed their reign, our politicians lowered the duties, and it was with difficulty sufficient protection was left on to keep alive the establishments that we had induced into existence.   The doctrine of free trade was so prevalent that we were prevented going on to wealth and comfort, and have ever since warred upon the manufacturing interest, in a way to almost paralyze it. The protection left on, however, has done wonders, and been worth millions to the nation, both in value, quality, comfort, and independence. A fortiori, since we succeeded in the handicraft, could we succeed much better in branches requiring machinery, since labor-saving aids do much in equalizing labor. The progress already made in manufacturing, the millions annually made or saved to the nation by our present operations, the independence and comfort derived from them, and the assurance that the extent already given to manufacturing is the effect of a protecting tariff, should encourage us to go on still further, and espouse the doctrine of protection as one already proved, and calculated to render us independent and rich. Protection is, therefore, our best policy, and due to our enterprising and industrious population.

CHAPTER V.

FREE TRADE.

THERE is something fascinating, but deceptive, in the idea of free trade. It seizes upon the unthinking, and takes with all that do not reflect; because it seems to be a sort of adjunct or corollary of liberty, in its broad and unrestrained sense. The dema-

gogues and designing politicians catch at popularity by using this popular term, and ring upon it all
the changes to suit their purposes. Let us examine for one moment the facts and circumstances of
this country in reference to its intercourse with
other nations, to enable us to understand the term
" free trade." I will here merely embrace its general rules or principles, and apply them to the
actual condition of the nations of the world, which
must be regarded in deciding the question of free
trade. Nations must be similarly circumstanced,
stand on the same footing, and have all advantages
and circumstances equal, in order to ensure the
principles of free trade working mutually beneficial to all. Any difference in their condition ; any
vantage ground ; any engrossing of skill, capital,
tonnage, or seamen ; any long established organization, would give to a nation possessing them the
vantage ground, and enable it to put all others under contribution, unless countervailed. Old nations
would, through it, subsidize young ones. A high
degree of manufacturing skill and refinement
would enable the nation having it to keep a hold
on all the world. A fertile and virgin soil in a
suitable climate, would be able to feed old worm-
eaten countries, and keep them always poor.

I will exemplify the above assumptions by a
few cases and facts, taken from real history and
from the nations with which we trade. The bulk
of our trade is with England. She is far advanced

in manufactures, in possession of all the skill, preparations, an unlimited capital, and a widely extended commerce. If there were no protecting duties, a perfectly free trade between us and England,
she would prostrate all of our manufactories in a single year. If she could not do it by skill, she would
by dint of her capital and commerce, and in one of
the following ways. She manufactures for her foreign customers, of every sort of thing, two hundred
million dollars worth a year. Suppose she has sold
annually one hundred and eighty millions for her
usual profit, and has twenty millions left of inferior
or refuse goods. Rather than have this balance
left on hand, she will sell them for whatever they
will bring. Where, I will ask, would she sell these,
and make her great sacrifice ? Not at home, to
affect her standard market, but abroad, where the
sacrifice would prostrate and produce convulsions
among us her rivals, who had but little capital, and
destroy our home market, which in all countries
must be the main market. She would not feel the
loss on these twenty millions, but they would be of
magnitude enough to ruin us. This sweeping off the
old stock, and cleaning out the warehouses and
shelves, is a thing of universal practice among merchants ; and whether there be a design in it or not
would make no difference, for the effect would be
the same on our manufactories. Again, if she did
it not in the way just named, she, by dint of her
capital, could well afford to raise and expend mil-

lions a year to keep down such a rival as we might become, and retain such a customer. When you add to the above her high vantage ground, her great skill, unlimited capital, low wages, cheap and extended tonnage, and agents and facilities planted every where to aid her operations, you may take it for granted that she would keep her ground and make us ever subservient.

Suppose a free trade between the Baltic and England in provisions? The greater cheapness of corn in the North of Europe would prostrate English agriculture in one or two years. Nothing but her corn laws prevents this. That great interest in England, built up by the restrictive system in her corn and provision culture, would be thrown to the four winds, and convulsions ensue. Would France, Belgium, and the North of Italy ever allow fancy goods to be made in any country without a restrictive system? Many other cases might be brought up to prove the utter impossibility of any young country, or one behind in skill and other advantages, ever coming up to an equality with old experienced nations.

Had our corn and provisions gone into England alone free of duty for the last forty years, it would have been worth not less than one thousand million dollars to us. We would certainly have sold not less than two million barrels of flour, worth ten million dollars, and as much or more of other provisions, each year to her; and we could

have easily spared that much. Who among nations now has the presumption to preach up free
trade ? England, emphatically, and under circumstances that ought to shame her. Without letting
our provisions in at all worth talking about, unless
she be starving ; after taxing our tobacco twelve
hundred per cent. ; our rice four hundred per cent. ;
and after taxing nearly all articles of manufacture to prohibition ; seated on her high vantage
ground, arrogating superiority from her capital and
naval supremacy, she has the presumption to
preach up to us free trade. She don't mean that
she must or will take off her duties, except in the
case of a few articles of manufactured goods ; and
leaving on all her corn laws, would reciprocate
with us only in such articles as she had the start
and skill in, and where, through her capital in the
way above named, she could prostrate us. Such
presumption is intolerable, and tantamount to insult. Whenever free trade hereafter be suggested,
it will either be from old advanced notions based
on interest, or from designing politicians expecting
to make capital out of the idea by humbugging the
ignorant. I feel assured that the idea in this country has nothing to do with patriotism.

Free trade has been the eternal cry of our noisy
politicians, and they have managed to engage in it
a large and almost dominant party in this country,
including most of the slave holders and staple districts. No one pretends to an equality among na-

tions, nor can it exist in the nature of things. Some nations stand on the vantage ground in every respect, as regards labor, capital, ships, productions, manufactures, and skill, as we have said. They have gotten the start of others in a way that can't be mistaken. Whether this be the effect of long time, superior skill, more capital, greater activity or wisdom in their councils, matters not; we look to the fact, and if it exists we must govern ourselves accordingly. I contend, all nations that have the vantage ground and this start, will not only keep them, but make them still more available and striking the longer time it runs, as snow-balls gather in size the farther they roll, or gravity increases in momentum and celerity the farther a body falls. England, for instance, with the start she has got, could put the whole world under contribution, and keep it so, if she met no obstruction. She would not only take entire possession of the new world, and the Indies, including China, but of Europe itself. She would clothe France and Holland, and Germany, and Italy, as well as all other countries, with her coarse cotton goods, and flood them with the thousands of things got up by dint of her machinery, capital, and skill, in the cheap way. There would be no limit to her operations, but the want of means in other nations to buy with. France and the Baltic also would prostrate the English agriculture, as we have said, and what they left America would finish. It may have

taken ages to place a nation on this vantage
ground, but the leverage that would give her
would enable her to keep it. Like two individuals
struggling in a narrow pass, the one who stood uppermost would beat back the one below; or as
two bodies meeting, of different sizes and momenta,
the largest will drive back the other. Make trade
free, let mankind buy where they can the cheapest,
and a few nations will master all, and absorb the
capital of the whole world. Who are the advocates for free trade? England, Holland, France,
and others, who can produce things, of the manufacturing class particularly, cheaper than others.
They would then feel that the world was made for
them, and proceed to take possession of it accordingly. The nations who got the start in each
thing would keep it, under this system; England,
the cotton goods, cutlery, and iron; France, the
silks; China, tea and china-ware; America and
the Baltic, grain; Ireland, linen; Turkey, fine
shawls and carpets; the Dutch, toys; Russia,
hemp; the Indies, sugar; United States, tobacco;
France, wine; and all other things as the advantage of each country or the start it has in the production of them warranted. The furnishing nation
would supply up to the wants or the ability of the
one furnished, as the case might be. Nations therefore are under an absolute necessity of countervailing each other, and laying on duties and protecting tariffs high enough to ensure the home market

to their own industry.   England, with her advantages and capital, may well cry aloud for free
trade, for she will profit most by it.   She may well
put arguments into her customers' mouths, and even
write tracts and distribute them among ignorant
people, who are waking up to their own interests,
to the reality of their situation, and would fain arrest
the impoverishing process before it be too late.
England, lately, when she had got all the capital or
money of the United States for goods that they
ought to have made at home, and finding the thing
growing slack, gave her credit for a year or two of
supply ahead.   She even loaned the States two hundred million dollars to stimulate them to do any sort
of things, for England knew that if that money should
be wasted there, it would nevertheless find its way
back to her, as an ability to buy more goods,
which it did in the most literal and absolute way.
A great deal of that money, indeed nearly all of it,
was realized through exchanges, in the shape of
goods bought in England and brought out to this
country for the laborers and their employers, to
pay them instead of money for their worthless
work on the roads and canals.   I have passed hundreds of miles through States that had been spending millions in making works and banking on these
English loans, and have seen scarcely a vestige of
improvements, except some empty unfinished dig-
gings.   These millions ran back to England so
rapidly for goods, that they had not touched a sin-

gle spring of industry, built a town, or even a house, except some board shanties in which to sell these goods and liquors. All the loose capital in the shape of money, leaves any country that buys its supplies from abroad. This money, being in hand and ready, offers an easy means of paying for them, and proves that the more money a nation that buys abroad possesses, the worse for her. Free trade therefore would be gain and great wealth to some few nations, but poverty and death to most of them.

CHAPTER VI.

POWER TO PROTECT.

THERE are politicians in our country hardy and reckless enough to deny the power or right to protect or lay restrictive duties. It is pretended that the Constitution of the United States gives no such power, or if it does allow imposts, yet it is meant for revenue alone, not for protection. Of all the bold and far-fetched constructions of this instrument, except perhaps the absurd doctrine of nullification, this is the most barefaced. The power is given directly to lay impost duties, and why confine it to revenue, any more than to manufactures or commerce? Were it not thus given, it would appertain to the power to take care of the general welfare, or to establish commerce, and even to the vital existence of a nation. I take all this as party spirit—as an effort to say something for effect with the ignorant, who once were taught by true patriots of the Washington stamp to reverence that instrument. No one will seriously question the right all nations have to encourage either manufactures, agriculture, or commerce, as circumstances favor the one or the other. No one will question the right a nation has to offer bounties or lay protecting duties intended to ensure the production of any article of luxury or necessity, or what might be necessary to the independence of the country. No one will seriously question the right that one nation has to countervail another that may pass some restriction that would lead to the injury of her commerce, or bear injuriously upon her.

To deprive a nation of the right to encourage her industry and her arts, to develope all or any of her resources, or to meet other nations on equal terms, would cripple her very existence. This doctrine would strike at her vitals, and throw her bound hand and foot into the power of her enemies. She could not then be independent, could not advance her prosperity, or aim at wealth and comfort. The very right to preserve her existence and independence, would imply such a power. It would appertain to her as a nation, and without it she would be but a province of other powers, and a foot-ball.

All the practice of the government, from the ratification of the federal Constitution up to this time, has been in favor of such a power. The acts of congress, the decisions of the federal court, the intercourse with foreign nations, the continued collections of our imposts, have all been in support of the power. The authority of our greatest politicians, from Washington the father of his country, and Hamilton the ablest and most practical politician that we ever had, including Mr. Jefferson, Mr. Madison, and even Gen. Jackson, have vouched the authority. Is it not strange that there should be any party, or set of politicians, at this day, after all the facts, and practice, and action of the government that we have named, with all this staring them in the face, bold enough or unprincipled enough to still assert the unconstitutionality of the power and deny its existence? The doubtful policies and principles of all nations become settled by such grave decisions, such high authorities, such continuous practices, and it is right that they should be so disposed of and settled. Our parties, however, obey no authority, regard no decisions, however solemn, submit to no practices or usages, no matter how long kept up and how deliberately made. They seem to wish to keep all afloat, to have all in doubt, to favor their designs and any unprincipled course aimed at. One of the worst features of our politics is this uncertain, varying, distracted state of things, and points strongly to anarchy and confusion. The steadiness of a government, and the justness of its administration depend much on having all great policies fixed, all doubtful principles settled, and some sacred tribunal to which to appeal in disputed cases. Since the authority of the federal court has been questioned, as it is by a large and powerful party, there seems to be no arbiter, nothing to stay the ruthless hands of party innovation, and give confidence and stability.

CHAPTER VII.

MANUFACTURES.

THE great interests of this country are Agriculture, Commerce, Manufactures, the Fisheries, the Currency, and the Forests, or Lumber. As the country at this time is most excited about manufactures, and lays the greatest stress on that interest, I shall first treat of that, and consider whether it requires any aid from the government or not. The power and right to protect being undoubted, it becomes a question of policy whether that great interest should be left to individual exertions, in other words, to chance; or call down the attention and protection of the government, to ensure its proper success and development. Circumstances,

as I have said before, must determine. I do not
hesitate one moment to declare it as my most de-
liberate opinion, as well as that of the wisest politicians of the nation, that our present circumstances
do favor a more extended system of manufactures,
and do require the protection of the government
in many branches, until fast established. The success attendant upon what we have already done
under a fair protection, and the wide-spread operations of our handicraft mechanics, warrant the
conclusion that, in other and greater branches,
with a fair protection, we would also succeed, and
not only enrich the country, but render it comfortable and independent. It is our best and leading
policy to so encourage and protect, and becomes
our bounden duty as a nation. In order to prove
that our circumstances do sufficiently favor manufactures to warrant a protective tariff, I will show
that we have an abundance of labor, capital,
capacity, raw materials, fuel, iron, water power,
demand, climate, facility of intercommunication,
cheap provisions, savings in freight, commissions,
storage, mean profits, and cost of materials, from
all which we would have vantage ground over all
other nations. With all these advantages, we
should not hesitate in making them available, up to
our own wants at least.

First : Surplus Labor. We need only to open
our eyes to be convinced of this fact. Nothing
strikes a foreigner so forcibly, on his arrival in this

country, as the great number of idle persons, young and old, male and female, that he sees in every city, village, or settlement, lounging and dissipating in a way to show that they have nothing on earth to do. This proves the fact, in a general point of view, that there is surplus labor. I will show this fact of surplus labor, however, more specially and more in detail. The census and our own observations prove that three-fourths of the whole population are engaged in agriculture, and most of them producing provisions, or rather live in the provision-growing districts. It is admitted that the profits of corn, wheat, pork, beef, flour, cheese, butter, lard, rice, potatoes, and all vegetables and eatables, are very small, and the market very limited for them. They can sell only a certain quantity to foreign countries, because those countries take them only as they are obliged to have them, to avoid suffering and starvation. It is admitted by all, both the people concerned in growing these provisions and the politicians, the political economist and the thousands of newspapers spread among them, that this provision-growing population could produce three times as much as it now does, if it had market enough, and the proper inducement. Hence they are all the time abusing England and other countries, for closing their ports against our provisions, and their restrictive laws or tariffs. About the year 1802, when scarcity and wars opened the ports of Europe for a year or two to our provisions, we did produce more than double our usual quantity, under even that doubtful inducement. These facts prove that there are too many laborers in the provision department of our agriculture, and that less than half can produce all that could be sold. The others are working slack, and a clog upon the whole operation. It proves that the products are already too great and overdone; that they are groaning under the burthensome accumulation of provisions, actually spoiling on hand for the want of a market. The great complaint of the farmer is, " we have no market," and are weighed down by our granaries, barns, store-houses, and dairies. Go to the great West, where fertility is without limit, and talk with the farmers; they will tell you of their evils, and point significantly to their overloaded fields and barns. Urge them to greater agricultural efforts, they will laugh in your face, and think you an ignoramus. They will tell you that they are raising hog and hominy, to use a western phrase, and eating them, and making linseys and wearing them, and are independent without money, a market, or refinement.

I will then assume the fact, and there are abundant proofs of it, that one-third of the laborers now engaged or living in the provision districts can grow all that a market can be found for. In other words, had they markets and a proper inducement, could grow three times as much as they now do, without any over-effort. This proves that our agricultural

department can spare all the labor wanted for manufactures. Twelve millions being engaged in this
pursuit, counting old and young, and one half old
and strong enough to be daily laborers, could well
spare one million, counting the proper proportion
of women and children, for manufacturing purposes,
and make none the less of provisions. Taking our
data from Lowell and some other of the most comfortable, orderly, and productive establishments in
the world, we see that full three-fourths of the
operatives are women and children. This shows
that a large proportion of the able-bodied hands
could still be left on the farms for rough and heavy
work. Light hands in a factory, particularly women,
are just as productive as men, and thus ensure a
wider and more extended productiveness, according to population, than agriculture ever could make
available.

Again, there are in and about our cities, towns,
and villages, thousands of idle persons producing
nothing, amounting, if women and children be
counted, to not less than half a million. These
people are not only not producing, but what is
worse, dissipating, contracting bad habits, and cor-
rupting others for the want of employment. They
might be induced to go to work, were an opportunity afforded to them. The families of fishermen,
whalers, and sailors, and also of the numerous travelling agents, merchants, and runners, might furnish
much labor to any manufactory in their neighbor-

hood, and be made available. Labor thus abstracted from the cities, from agriculture and other pursuits, would leave nothing impaired; the rather would unclog and ameliorate, and render more virtuous, happy, and comfortable, not only the laborers thus abstracted, but the departments from which they should be taken.

Should all these sources of labor fail to furnish enough, which is very improbable, there is still another wide field to enter, that is untouched, and that could easily furnish three or four hundred thousand laborers. I mean the slaves that are not engaged in the heavy staple cultures. Maryland, Virginia, Kentucky, Tennessee, North Carolina, Missouri, and other districts entirely out of the sugar, cotton, tobacco, and hemp regions, have 1,500,000 slaves engaged in the provision districts, whose labor is but of little profit to their owners. According to the proportions above established, one third of these slaves can grow all the provisions that the whole are now producing. More than half could therefore be spared for other operations, without affecting, otherwise than favorably, their present pursuits. Not less than 300,000, then, could be turned to manufactures, under the proper inducement. Let it not be here said that slaves would not do for manufacturers, for experience and facts prove it untrue. Wherever the negro slave has been put to, or entrusted with, manufactories, he has showed himself both trustworthy and efficient.

Twenty thousand cotton gins, by enumeration, exist in the cotton districts of the United States, and are all in the care and management, in a manner, of slaves; and many are constructed by them, particularly the buildings and gearings. These are very delicate machines, very dangerous ones, and easier destroyed by fire than any others, because the whole atmosphere in and about them is inflammable, from the flos cotton flying about; yet not more losses occur in them than in other manufactories in the United States. The number of houses and gins burned in the slave states do not exceed that of the free; and of all these 20,000 gins, not more than about ten are annually burned, which would not be one-fourth of one per cent. All the hemp manufactories in Kentucky and Missouri are carried on by slaves, from the growing and preparing the hemp, to the spinning and weaving, with complete success. Several cotton and woollen factories in Virginia, Kentucky, Tennessee, Georgia, Alabama, and the Carolinas, are carried on by negroes. The heaviest iron establishment in the United States, that of Yeatman, Woods & Co., Tennessee, is carried on by slaves, including the digging, roasting, coaling, refining, casting, naileries, rolling foundries, and machine shops appendant thereto, and all the skill of each department furnished by slaves. Many other establishments in the slave states are conducted in like manner by slaves; and most of the blacksmiths, shoemakers, carpenters, wagon-makers, and thousands of other handicraft employments in the south, are carried on by slaves, greatly to the comfort and wealth of the owners.

The negro slave is fitted by nature for an operative; is healthy, strong, steady in his nerves, and highly imitative in his habits. You own this labor, can regulate it, work it many or few hours in the day, accelerate or stimulate it, control it, avoid turnouts and combinations, and pay no wages. You can dress it plainly, feed it coarsely and cheap, lodge it on simple forms, as the plantations do, house it in cabins costing little, and all the skill you impart to it is your own, and not to enable it to rise up and extort on you as the free labor often does, and quit you in time of need. On the score of humanity, the slave is better off in a comfortable warm house in-doors, than exposed half clad on the farms, amid swamps and rain, and would be more cheerful and happy. Another view equally dear to humanity, and worth still more, is the idea of exempting to that extent free people, and particularly delicate females and children, from factory drudgery and labor. As we are destined to hold slaves through a series of years yet, perhaps a century or two, let us bestow upon them the worst, most unhealthy and degrading sort of duties and labor, to the exemption of free persons. This would shock humanity no more than slavery does, and make freedom more dignified and valuable.

There is another way of looking at this subject, that places it on a footing totally different from
all other kinds of labor. The slaves are owned,
and not regarded in the districts I speak of as capital. The owner will not sell them from the proper
feelings of humanity; nor will he free them, because he feels and knows that they would be in a
worse condition. He therefore stands in a curious
relation to his slaves, and a sort of tacit understanding exists between them, that, as long as the slave
can feed and clothe himself, the master will identify
himself with him. There are not less than half a
million of slaves in the United States in that situation, and on that footing. I am warranted, therefore, in pronouncing them no capital to their owners.
Suppose the slaves so circumstanced be put to manufacturing, for which we have showed above they
are well qualified, what will their wages be? The
elements of their wages to the owners would be
the food and clothing they consume, for unfortunately they more than insure themselves by their
increase. I can feed and clothe snugly, within
doors, and in a warm room, a slave for twenty dollars
a year, and in a way to be more comfortable than on
a plantation. Now divide twenty dollars among
three hundred working days in the year, and it is
about six and a quarter cents a day, the wages that
such labor would cost. In the free portions of the
United States such labor costs forty cents, and in
Europe from twenty to twenty-five cents a day.
Such a wide difference must count, and some day

turn the world upside down. All the advantages
are in favor of slave labor, and humanity also; except perhaps that in this mode productive slavery
might be prolonged and easier controlled.

We will now sum up as to the amount of surplus
or idle labor in this country, and see what might be
made available for manufacturing purposes. From
the agricultural districts one million; from the cities,
villages, marine and fishing districts, half a million;
from the slave districts, four hundred thousand; and
from other bye places, one hundred thousand:
making in all not less than two millions that might
be gathered up and made useful for manufacturing
or other new occupations. This abstraction would
leave agriculture in a much more wholesome condition, not only unclogged, but in possession of a new
and increasing market or demand, and a set of customers that would have the ability to consume. It
would also break up those dens of vice in our cities
and villages that are now sustained by the idle.
The above vast amount of labor would be greatly
increased from the very circumstance of protection
giving a certainty of employment, by bringing or
inducing thousands of the best and most skilful
laborers from Europe, and establishing them in this
country. No doubt, therefore, can remain as to the
abundance of labor in the United States to establish and work manufactories up to our own consumption. We have more available laborers than
England and this country both employ in the cotton,
woollen, iron, silk, and other large interests. Eng-

land employs in these branches not more than half a million laborers, and makes annually, including her own consumption, not less than four hundred million dollars worth. How overwhelming the idea, that we have idle people enough to produce four hundred million dollars a year! Confine it, however, to our own home supply only, yet we might save, by making it, the seventy or eighty million dollars worth of goods that we import from abroad, without in the least straining after foreign markets, or risking any thing at all. A protection that would secure to us our home market would save us this eighty millions a year, and soon enrich us. Applying any more labor to any branch of agriculture would be the utmost folly; it would be like the process of hammering a guinea; you may give to it more expansion, but no more value; indeed impair, the rather, its sterling stamp and character.

CHAPTER VIII.

CAPITAL.

LET us now inquire whether we have capital enough to give to this labor an outfit of machinery. As a proof that capital is abundant, interest in New-York and our other great cities is only four per cent., and great inquiries daily made for objects of investment, and anxieties continually manifested for the employment of capital. In circulation and banks, and on hand in individual coffers, there are, by the best official estimates, two hundred and fifty million dollars. Agriculture, even the planting and great staples, as well as the provision growing, affords too small profit to induce investment in it in any shape. Commerce is perhaps more overdone than agriculture, and offers as little inducement to capitalists to turn capital into it. The retail business is weighed down by competition, as well as the wholesale and importing; shipping is already too numerous, and freights too low to invite investments in that way; what stocks are good are bought up in England, and what are doubtful cannot induce real capitalists, scarcely the reckless speculators. Who that sees the country groaning under agricultural products, the parade of goods in all the streets of all the towns, and the doubtful character of most of the stocks, would invest in them? All the extension now given to agriculture is a case of necessity; simply for that sort of scant support and meagre independence that a farming life gives; to raise, as the western men say, hog and hominy, and mayhap, chickens and vegetables, and eat them; and spinning linsey, and wearing it. The two hundred and fifty millions above named, then, is without any permanent object of investment, and might be induced into any new channel of business, if a prospect of profit and permanency ran together. It might well be employed, under a protecting tariff, in machinery, and developing our iron and coal, or any other branches requiring an outfit of machinery and stock.

Should a judicious protecting tariff be passed by our congress, establishing a fixed policy, and offering sufficient inducement to manufacturers, not only our own capital would be turned in, but any amount that we might want would come from England. This would be the more desirable, because it would be an accumulation or addition to that amount, bring its skill with it, and go to work on a sure basis. Nothing is wanting to draw money from England, where it is worth only two or three per cent., but a permanency and stability in our policies and laws. We have every motive, therefore, to cease our versatile course, and settle down in a way to give confidence to our institutions and pursuits. Confidence, permanency, and profits, are all necessary to induce capitalists to invest and give their attention as well as their money.

Whenever a proper object presents itself, and a certainty of profit is held out in this country, an ingenious, thrifty people, such as we are, would never want capital, were it five times as scarce as it is. Profit is a magic creative term in this country, and calls up capital in the shape of credit, labor, and materials for preparation; and when the fixtures and machinery are made, the establishment carries itself on. Naked or mere labor, pledged under circumstances where almost certain profits await it, becomes capital, and serves until the profits return upon it in the shape of a realization. When credit is connected with a real transaction, and avoids speculation, it soon becomes the capital needed, and thus any vacuum in that respect is filled up and supplied. Credit and labor seem to double back on their own operations, and become all the reality of capital, as soon as some certainty be given to the prospect of profits. In verification of this, we will find many instances around us. When the growth of a city, for instance, requires more houses, they spring up like magic, and are the fruits of labor, with almost no capital in the shape of money. When the great West wanted 300 steamboats to meet its increasing commerce, and had not one dollar with which to build them, labor and materials came forward, aided by credit, and soon put the boats afloat, and that whilst the timid were wondering how it was to be done. So it would be in the case of manufactures, if the protection were given. I have seen a whole cotton crop in the south purchased by bills drawn on time or credit, and the cotton go forward and be sold to meet them, without any active capital being at all consumed in the operation.

Our banks have a wish at this time to do business, and make loans; and they would be ready to aid any safe and real transaction. They have suffered so much by speculators and adventurers, that they would naturally incline to favor any industrial operation going on in their neighborhood; and, with their positive means and unlimited credit, could furnish any amount of capital wanted for legitimate purposes. We are now on the upward spring of business, with much credit, and without any runs on banks, or want of confidence in each other; all which circumstances would draw money out of banks to any extent, for certain business, without creating any alarm, and also from such capitalists as did not choose to invest in manufacturing, and required interest only. The friends, therefore, of manufactures, have no fears as to the sufficiency of capital, if the protection were had, and a confidence lit up as to the permanency of the policy.

CHAPTER IX.

CAPACITY AND INTELLIGENCE.

THE citizens of the United States are noted for their practical shrewdness and inventive genius. The daily manifestations of skill and contrivance in executing difficult works, strike all who look abroad and witness such operations. The management and contrivance of the Yankees are proverbial, and their tact in bringing things to bear on or fit one another. They have more tact in getting up a business, more contrivance in carrying it on, and more invention to aid its operation, than any other people. New inventions, new machinery, and new principles, are continually announced. Godfrey, Rittenhouse, Fulton, Evans, Whitney, Whitmore, Reed, Brewster, Bigelow, and a hundred others, have added invaluable improvements to mechanics, and aids to labor. In all factories and shops, as well as in the patent office, do we find records and samples of these inventions in practical operation. No prejudice, or heavy previous investments in old forms, lie in the way of adopting all improvements here, and making them immediately available. We feel the necessity of using the best to enable us to compete with older nations, where wages are lower and more skill engaged. The English are slow to adopt any new invention; having three hundred millions invested in old machinery, they dislike to throw it away, and fear to change that fixed and monotonous habit which their operatives have got into, in connection with old machinery. The English proprietor goes for dividend, and knows nothing new, cares not for it, or studies its operation. The operatives under him are ground down to minimum wages, and with the heavy excise taxes upon them, can't stop to invent, or think enough about forms to strike out any new idea; indeed, reject all that are offered as hazardous, and likely to lead to some change or suspension of his wages.

Our free institutions give to the minds of our people much elasticity and independence of thought. They are habitually accustomed to inquire, examine every thing, and combine whatever materials they have to do with, in all ways most natural and effectual. This habit of inquiry and freedom of thought appertains to all, even the operator and common mechanic, who have not only this vigor of intellect thus cherished, but time to think and experiment much, because his wages are good and the means of living so certain and easy that he can afford to hazard something. It is generally the common mechanic or operator who is with and near the machinery that makes or suggests improvements, and most of the valuable patents and inventions issue from such persons.. A country of free institutions, unprejudiced feelings, and easy and cheap means of living, can afford to pause from intense daily operations to think and invent. An intelligence runs here with the mass, and imparts not only an aptitude for mechanical or factory operations, but gives character to the laborers, and leads to a confidence between the employers and the operatives that is worth much. Hence much of what is performed is job work, implying character and confidence, and stimulates the laborer to do nearly twice as much as the mere hireling. The character or quality of the laborers are worth as much or more than any difference in wages to the proprietors and the country. The English operator is a wagon horse, and a slow one at that, working moodily and slowly for his food and rags of clothing ; cares not for results, and has no spring, no hopes, no aspirations beyond the dull routine. This quality of our labor, based upon intellect and character, will put the world under contribution when rightly started, and working under a certainty of a market and a permanent policy.

We have the activity of body as well as of the mind to subserve us in manufacturing operations. Our people have an elastic spring, leading to much quickness and continuity in their action, and are more hardy, and can endure more than the English. Their greater quickness in action is manifested in handling things, such as arms, shooting, ship tackle, sailing ships, firing cannon, chopping wood, and any manufacturing operations requiring manipulation. We beat the world in sailing ships, fishing, and moving from place to place. In our manufactories often, English and Americans are both working together, and invariably do the natives execute more than foreigners, particularly in job work. This greater action arises in part from our climate, which is of a dry, sunny, exciting character; and from the sudden and continual changes, the constitution becomes tough, and the muscles elastic and pliant. We are not so round of limb, and of so full a person as the English, but have more of the active, hardy, available qualities. Our people eat more animal food, exercise more, live more in the open air, or out doors; and move over more space in transacting ordinary business than the Europeans, and thence acquire a quicker and more enduring action. The detached settlements of this country, obliges us to travel much and move over great space in transacting our business, embracing many remote points and changes in climate. At sea, Cape Horn is not even a resting-place; and China, South America, and Europe, common trading places. On land, from New Orleans to Maine, from New York to Missouri, from the upper lakes of Canada to Charleston and the Gulf, and the threading of our great western rivers and wide opening prairies, are common trips, undertaken annually by thousands of our commonest citizens, on some sort of business or speculation. The clearing away of our numerous forests, and the bulk of our population being engaged in agriculture, has contributed no little to this hardy and quick action. No matter whence it arises, we feel certain that we do possess it, and need only a fair opportunity, a proper inducement, to draw it out and make it available for national wealth and individual comfort. We intended the term capacity, in this chapter, to embrace our bodily and mental qualifications only, in regard to a successful manufacturing operation, and shall not crowd under it here any other aids and qualifications we may possess, or our country furnish, to aid the policy.

CHAPTER X.

RAW MATERIALS.

We have raw materials in great variety and of the best quality, in the United States, to aid the whole routine of manufacturing operations. The raw materials enter into such a business to the extent of one fourth of the capital employed, with Europeans living remote from them; and they have to keep, for their own safety, a stock on hand equal to that extent, which of course swells their capital, and is a disadvantage to them. When a people have all the raw materials in abundance around them, it seems to invite them to manufactures, if their circumstances suit, and to make it a sort of duty to work them up and avail themselves of them. The God of nature seems to have thrown them in their way for wealth and comfort; and if their politicians do not insure the proper employment of them they should stand condemned for a dereliction of their duty.

It never could be intended, in the nature of things, long at a time, that two freights, two storages, two commissions, and two profits, should be paid or sustained in any case, and ought not to be so. Take the case of cotton, which is grown here. It has to be put up by strong compression, perhaps injuring its quality; encounters a freight, storage, commission, profit, and a duty, in going out to England; and more and similar charges up to Manchester, and the same charges back again here, on its return in the shape of textures for our consumption. All these charges swell the cost of the raw material, which we would avoid in the main, and to that extent stand on the vantage ground over England.

We have cotton in unlimited quantity, and of the best quality, which is now a very important and leading raw material in the manufactures of the age.   No nation can compete with us in producing this article, and nothing. can occur to intercept its continued production or diminish its volume.   We can supply ourselves, and all other countries in addition, without any more effort or higher price. We have the climate, soil, skill, and the sort of labor suited to its culture, and, if we wished to do so, could not, dare not, quit its cultivation.   If we were to make the ten million dollars worth of cotton goods that we now import, it would only require about sixty thousand bales more of our cotton, out of a crop of two million bales, which would not much impair our export of the article, and would leave us enough to put Europe under contribution, for they must have it.   When I say that Europe must have our raw cotton, I mean that it is her interest to take it, because it will be the cheapest and best.   We will continue to grow it cheaper than any other people, and such will be the competition among the spinners of Europe, that no one will dare to give a bounty for cotton, or pay more for it than their neighbor, or lay a tax upon it.   Every pound of the raw cotton that we might spin under a proper protection will be our own ; and were we to impart the five additional values to the raw which the wrought amounts to, it would be all that clear, and done by a population that would be otherwise idle and producing nothing.

Innumerable are the advantages resulting from the possession of so valuable a raw material as cotton. Besides those named above, it would contribute no little to our independence as a nation, and put us in possession of an article by the aid of which we might paralyze Europe any year we pleased, or force from her any terms we might insist upon for the advantage of our shipping and commerce. I will speak more particularly hereafter of our cotton crop, and the influence it exerts upon our labor and income.

The raw material of iron is without limit also in this country, and stands in value perhaps even ahead of cotton. Iron is the right hand of human operations, and a sine qua non in fact in all the arts, comforts, and even luxuries of man. Did we not ourselves show the instance, I would have said no nation on earth is, or could be, inconsiderate enough, or so wanting to her own interests and independence as to import this indispensable article of human necessity. Tell an Englishman, or a Swede, or a Frenchman, or even a Russian, that such a nation exists, pretending to the arts and sciences, and a high degree of civilization and prosperity, and they would not suppose it possible, and scout the very idea. Every thing stands arrested at the very threshold of advancement without this very necessary aid—this Samson of the age —that supports all fabrics, from a plough up to a ship, a bridge, or a house, and takes the place of wood and stone in all our operations. It is equally necessary to the fine arts, and our comforts and luxuries in the small every day concerns and fixings. How could any nation—how did we dare go to war with a powerful nation—dare to put on a non-intercourse with the world, without this indispensable raw material? When I speak of iron as a raw material in abundance, I mean the ore, which lies unwrought in the bowels of the earth, whilst our wise politicians are importing from Europe nearly one half that we use. There is scarcely a state in this Union, except the alluvial of Louisiana, and the flat prairies of Illinois, but has plenty of iron ore. Mountains of it lie untouched in Missouri; the compass will not traverse for it in parts of Arkansas, Tennessee, Kentucky, Pennsylvania, New-York, New-Jersey, Vermont, New-Hampshire, Maryland, Virginia, particularly, show it in quantities that would serve the whole world for ages, and of a quality unsurpassed. No deep mining or drifting becomes necessary to work it; lying on the surface every where, it seems to invite attention: From New England to Arkansas, from the Northern Lakes to the Gulf, from Pennsylvania to Missouri, it abounds; and along side of it the fuel and other facilities to work it. The reason that we do not work iron up to our want without protection is, the large capital it requires for furnaces, blasts, ore beds, fuel, and much machinery of a complicated and particular sort, and the want of skill necessary to the operation. Our independence as a nation, as well as our interests and comforts, is immediately concerned in the abundant supply of iron; and our government should immediately insure its production, by a duty high enough and permanent enough to satisfy all, and leave no doubt of success. This age more than the past cries aloud for iron, because the application of it is endlessly varied. That nation that has not iron, or pays two prices for it, is sure to be thrown aback in the great progress of the arts and of civilization. Those who possess it will pass her by, and laugh at the folly that placed or kept her in that condition. Iron, more iron, give us iron, is the cry of all who aim to ameliorate the condition of man, or make useful and permanent improvements.

We have fuel of every sort in any abundance, which is in the nature of a raw material, or at least it subserves the manufacturing of all raw materials. Our forests are in a manner unbroken, and furnish charcoal or crude wood without price, for all the purposes to which it may be applicable, and always right alongside of the iron, lead, and copper. Centuries will not make scarce this common and primitive fuel, which for certain operations answers better than stone coal, particularly in making tough bar iron. These forests spread before the door of every individual; from which he derives comfort and warmth; and surround every manufacturing village with their facilities and comforts. Stone coal underlays nearly one fifth part of the United States. You may travel in the West fifteen hundred miles in length by five hundred in breadth over a bituminous coal mine of the very best sort and easily got at, frequently without any mining or sinking a shaft, because it stares you in the face above the lowest levels of the country. Many detached beds of the same are found near Richmond in Virginia, Cumberland in Maryland, and Blossberg in Pennsylvania, large enough for the supply of ages. Anthracite abounds in Pennsylvania, lying above the ground in mountain masses of the best and purest sort, and inexhaustible in quantity. Coal at the mine can be delivered for sixty cents to a dollar a ton, and carried cheaply to any point where it may be wanted. The manufacturing villages should be located at the entrance to the mines, where fuel will always be at minimum prices. Nations in the world are advanced, and wealthy or powerful, exactly in proportion as they work and develope their coal and iron. England has put the whole world under contribution by her coal and iron, and has made money enough to purchase the half of mankind if she chose.

We have lead in more abundance than any portion of the globe, and have fortunately worked and developed it without any further protection, for the simple reason that it required very little capital or skill to prepare it. An Irishman or Yankee digs it with his hands, and smelts it upon fires made with logs of wood, without any assistance from skill or capital. The case of iron and lead shows us, in a strong and convincing way, the difference in getting up something without skill and capital, and another thing requiring both ; the one will be done like the handicrafts, and the other left undone until protection gives the proper inducement. We are now not only producing lead up to our own wants, but exporting a great deal of it to Europe, and even to China.

We have plenty of copper ore in Illinois, Missouri, and Michigan, and are beginning to work it. This operation is slow, because it requires more skill and capital to mine for it and smelt it than the lead business ; hence we wait for a protection that will promise permanency. On the shores of Lake Superior there is said to be copper enough for the world. As soon as ordinary manufactures gain protection and confidence enough to start, this copper will be found ready to aid them as a raw material to any extent, and, as lead, may become an article for export.

We have all the salts constituting the raw material, particularly the alkalis, saltpetre, alum, copperas, common salt of soda; and they could be soon combined into the shapes wanted for manufactures, including the acids.

We have the marbles of every variety and beauty, the limestones, the granites, the slates, the magnesias, the gypsums, the silex or sand, and the clays, such as the alumina for the acids and salts, the kaolins for fine wares, the plastic and fire clays for all purposes. The acids, the gases, and salts

can all be made here to subserve any quantity of
manufactures that we may enter upon, and most
probably for export.

We have gold in quantity, covering five hundred
miles square, and mixing in the soil; some silver,
plenty of cobalt and zinc, and many precious stones
worth working into the arts. This native gold being pure, is suited to the arts better than coin,
which is mixed with alloy. Tin is the only useful
metal that is not yet found in this country, and
would constitute the only exception to the long
catalogue of things necessary to the most extended
manufactures, unless diamonds be reckoned.

Besides woods for fuel, we have a great and unlimited variety of them for the arts, and particularly for the cabinet-maker, carriage-maker, house-
joiner, ship-builder, and even for the construction of
the smaller ornamental articles of luxury. The
dye-stuffs, to a great extent, are found naturally
growing, and should our manufactures start into a
capital existence, pari passu with them, and, as a
part of the system, indigo, madder, woad, cochineal,
and the earths so used, would be immediately produced, not only for the demand, but for exportation.

We have wool, or can have it, in abundance.
Already the cultivation of that article nearly meets
our wants, and, having all the varieties of sheep
now under cultivation, it can soon swell up to any
demand, and leave a large surplus for exportation.
We see, therefore, that the same stimulus that

would start manufactures, would give an impulse
to many raw materials even for exportation, after
supplying the home market.   We have also fur,
collected from a wide extent of country, extending
across the Rocky Mountains to the very Pacific.
Hair, also, and bristles, and whalebone, abound here
as raw materials, subserving many of the arts in
a way to meet even the luxuries of a people.

We are now commencing the silk culture, and
have already proved that we can grow it of a better quality than Europe, and to any extent.   The
climate favors the insect, as well as the mulberry
tree upon which it feeds.   A little more inducement would pour forth silk enough to clog the markets of the world, after meeting our own wants,
and, very probably, without such further inducement it will be done.   This culture does not require
much capital, and the skill is soon acquired.   On
the principle of the handicrafts, therefore, it will
succeed, and engage the labor of women and children, without calling them off from their farms and
houses, as other manufactures would have to do,
in order to secure their services, and be for that
reason preferred.

We have the lints to any extent, particularly
flax and hemp, and are already doing much in their
production, especially the latter, and in the working of it up into fabrics.   Flax grows well, and besides its lint furnishes to the arts the oil and cake.

We have all the oils, and lard, and sperm, and
stearin, already produced for export, and standing

ready to subserve any extent of manufacturing operations or the arts that may be instituted, for lights, lubrication, ordinary grease, or any combination that they may enter into. These materials are cheaper and more abundant in this country than any other, and are now exported to a great extent.

We have tobacco, which is a raw material in many respects, and sugar and rice, which enter into many operations requiring the art of the manufacturer or chemist. The medicinal vegetables grow well here, such as rhubarb, the castor bean, jalap, senna, and many others. In all abundance we have alcohol and spirits, and all the grains suited to beer and to them. All the above enumerated long list of raw materials are so universally distributed, that every district either possesses them or lies in reach of them; and on all would the saving of freights, storages, commissions, profits, and insurances, that we spoke of above, be saved in a way to give signal advantages to our manufacturers over all others. These raw materials will be in better order, and in a sounder condition, when used fresh and near the place where produced, than after encountering long sea voyages, and damps, and dirt, incident to much handling and rolling about. The cotton, particularly, after the high pressure necessary to a European voyage, has to be at some expense opened out with pickers, and restored to its flos state and life again.

CHAPTER XI.

PROVISIONS, WATER POWER, TAXES, POOR LAWS, MACHINERY.

WE have provisions more abundant, cheaper, and of a better quality in this country, than any other in the world. This is no small advantage in manufacturing operations. The operatives are comfortable and happy, and can work, if necessary, cheaper where provisions are so cheap and abundant, than in countries differently circumstanced. We would be saved that continual distress that the laborers of Europe are subjected to, by the scarcity and high price of provisions. Good order and contentment in the operatives work well in manufactures, and render labor doubly efficient. The aid that our teeming agriculture would give to our manufacturers, would be deeply felt in the realization of comfort, good order, and happiness among the operatives ; and would, as now at Lowell, present scenes that would please instead of shock humanity or the moralist.

In no country does water power more abound than in the United States. As it costs less than steam power for heavy and permanent operations, it would give us much advantage. At the head of

navigation in all our rivers, from Maine to Alabama, and immediately connected with health, ship
or steamboat navigation, there are falls in all our
rivers; at each of which, not less than fifty, might
a Manchester be built, as far as power is concerned. In the West also they abound, particularly near
Pittsburgh, Cincinnati, Zanesville, Akron, Dayton,
Rock Island, on Rock River, Fox River, Desmoines,
Osage, Muscle Shoals of Tennessee, Harpeth, and
on the Wabash River. These powers are of the
best, most permanent, and easily applied. Most of
these water privileges, too, are in regions noted for
their fertility, and affording a large consuming population near them; and, as we have said, have navigation facilities to carry off the goods and bring
the raw materials to their proper markets.

The expenses of our government are infinitely
less than in England and France, and of course
taxes must be in proportion in the two countries.
Our taxes are not high enough to become excise,
or to reach the poll in this country; and, falling on
real estate or capital, are less felt by laborers. In
England, a vast weight of this taxation becomes
excise, and falls on the poor and operatives, and
must not only affect wages but comforts in a
great degree. In working down wages in that
country to the minimums, from excessive competition, they must leave enough for bare subsistence,
and in the ascending scale meet this millstone of
taxation that hangs around the necks of all. The
grinding taxation of the government is heard and

felt as much or more in proportion in the hovels of the poor, in their wages, than in the halls of the rich. All this difference, therefore, in the burthens of the two countries, in the prices of provisions and the costs of raw materials, redounds to the advantage of this country, and places us conspicuously on the vantage ground.

The poor laws and tithes of England are a further burthen, on the capitalist particularly. When the proprietors of the manufacturing villages and cities of that country come to add, at the end of the year, the thousands that they pay to broken down operatives, who all gain a parish settlement, and the charity necessary to the support of turn-outs and suspension or slack working of their mills, it no little swells the amount of wages. Scarcely any of the operatives in England realize any thing for old age, and, when it comes, lean on the poor rates. Thousands of them have no providence or saving qualities, even if their wages admitted of it, because they spend it all in drink. Not only the men, but women and children, attend the gin-shops of nights and Sundays, and spend their last cent, until they not only become fit subjects for a poor-house, but hospitals. They contract the habit until they are sots, if they have surplus pennies enough to enable them to do it, and then become thrown out of employment, but still are subjects for the poor laws and charities. This habit not only adds to the burthens of taxes, but deeply affects the quality and character of the labor in that country; for you will see men at work, stupid from the revels of the over night or Sunday, sullen and morose, caring nothing for the interests of the employer, and giving no character to their work. It is widely different in America, where active, smart men and women, with substance and character at home, go into the factories, and give character to every operation. They are educated, religiously moral, truthful, trustworthy, and, by doing job-work, earn more wages in the day in pushing the work and giving close attention. They save money, realize wealth, and increase their comforts, sufficiently to enable most of them to establish themselves in society with respectability. They never think of poor-rates, and by their character are placed entirely above them. This difference in the labor of the two countries is worth millions.

Machinery tends to equalize labor and wages. The Americans are proverbial for their inventions in machinery, and their tact in adopting any and all improvements made, and having them of the very best sort and latest invention. When a five hundred horse-power works in aid of human labor, requiring only a few to attend it, and doing the work of a thousand, the wages of the few attendants, however they may differ in the detail, become of little consequence in the grand operation. In such a case, we look to results rather than small differences, and place the American alongside of the Englishman. Rents, too, are higher in England than in this country, and become an increased

charge on both labor and capital. When we come
to sum up and realize all these advantages, they more
than make up any difference in the mere wages of
the two countries, and place us decidedly on the
vantage ground in regard to manufacturing operations.

CHAPTER XII.

FACILITIES OF COMMERCE, INTERCOMMUNICATIONS, AND INTERCHANGES IN AID OF MANUFACTURES.

THE commerce of the United States is active
and well organized; and stands ready to aid manufactures, in bringing to them the raw material and
provisions, and in carrying off and distributing
the goods to the consuming markets, at home and
abroad. This commerce takes up the foreign and
coasting trade with equal facility, despatch, and
cheapness, and becomes active or enlarged, as required for any legitimate purpose. We have per-
fected also many long lines of intercommunication,
by railroads, canals, and steamboat lines: thus
giving all possible facility to our internal trade and
home market. These, like the arteries of the system, diffuse wealth and trade every where, and
carry supplies of provisions, raw materials, and
manufactured goods wherever wanted or consumed.

The articles made thus, without accumulation, or much expense or delay, find their ultimate market. These gigantic works connect the raw material districts with the manufacturing—the producing districts with the consuming—the Atlantic states with the Mississippi valley—the northern lakes with the Gulf of Mexico; reducing transportation to the minimum, and enabling every part of the interior to procure and consume up to their ability. Such a system stimulates not only production, but promotes consumption, by throwing all within the reach of all; and carries a creative influence along with it to the very Ultima Thule, to originate new cultures, develope new resources, and increase both production and consumption. It brings things into value and usefulness that lay untouched before such a facility was extended, and widely enlarges our available means.

These intercommunications establish a system of beautiful trade and interchanges throughout the whole extent of the United States. This system works free and brotherly: no revenue laws or imposts lie across its free paths and open channels, to avert or interrupt its current of trade. No vexatious custom-house crew to overhaul parcels, question invoices, and worry all concerned. Each state and district barters freely with its neighbors, pours forth its productions, and realizes its wants *ad libitum*. The tide of commerce and trade, swelled by a thousand tributary streams that continually flow in, acquires an overwhelming current—fertilizing

and enriching all as it flows onwards. Distance is
nothing, and time scarcely estimated in such a rapid interchange, that like the sun sheds forth its
light and heat, vivifying all; not a wandering, flar-
ing, uncertain comet, that appears once in an age,
and brings alarm and disease rather than health
and cheerfulness. The United States, by these
aids, will be to each other what the several nations
of Europe might be to one another, without any
restrictive systems, custom-houses, countervailing
laws, and cherished jealousies.

   Let us regard a picture of these states, in brotherly feeling mutually dependent upon each other,
all united, and enriching each other by a mutual
interchange of wants and productions. Nothing
in the prospective can more delight the patriot than
such a scene—such a pledge of prosperity and comfort. The different districts and states through
such a medium will pour forth their peculiar products into the great mart. Louisiana its sugar and
indigo; the Carolinas, Georgia, Alabama, and Mississippi, their mighty volume of cotton; Kentucky
and Virginia their tobacco; Missouri and Kentucky,
hemp ; Illinois, Iowa, and Missouri, lead and copper ; Ohio, West New York and Pennsylvania,
flour, wheat, butter, cheese, and live stock; the
newer states along with Ohio, pork, lard and beef;
Vermont, the hills of New England and Pennsylvania, wool and silk; New England, New York,
and Pennsylvania, manufactured goods in every
variety ; Pennsylvania and the West, coal and iron,

and the manufactures based upon them; North Carolina and Maine, lumber; New York, foreign goods and productions; New England, their fisheries; the Far West, its furs. All places, districts, and corners will send out what they may have peculiar or surplus; whether of agricultural, manufacturing, commercial, mining, or the forest productions; whether of nature or art. How grand will roll on the tide of wealth and trade! how pleasing and absorbing the very contemplation of such a scene! the lights and shadows of such a picture!

It would seem to convince a stranger that a nation that had done so much for its internal trade, and the intercourse of the people, was deeply engaged in manufacturing and supplying its own wants through such mediums. What would be the surprise, however, when told that all this was done to facilitate foreign trade, and to let into our very bosom all foreign articles of manufacture! We shall have been working for foreigners unless we protect our own industry sufficiently to avail ourselves of these works. As things now stand we give all possible facility to the introduction of foreign goods that we ought to make ourselves; and not only invite them by low duties to our shores, but diffuse them to every part in a certain and cheap way. We have taxed ourselves hundreds of millions to make these canals and railroads, to let strangers enjoy them, and through them to paralyze our industry and draw from our very bowels our last cent. We have been working for others; have been straining our credit,

making debts and loans enough to both disgrace us
and grind down our posterity into the very dust for
the benefit of other nations. Instead of our own
articles and goods being carried on them, we open
them to strangers, whom we meet in the remotest
interior, not only availing themselves of our works
to prostrate our industry with their goods, but laughing at our simplicity, insulting our forbearance, and
claiming to have us for eternal customers. The debts
the states have contracted abroad, unless counteract-
ed by encouraging our own industry at home, will
reduce us to mere colonies of England for the next
age. Paying twelve or fifteen millions interest abroad
annually will take all our surplus money, and leave
nothing for an increased wealth or comfort; fifty
millions paid and expended at home would not be
half as much felt, nor produce half the stagnation
and privation. In such payments there is no remead,
no return made of the money thus gone for ever. it
doubles not back upon the exhausted country, and
touches no new springs of industry to atone for the
loss; unlike the home expenditures, no matter how
heavy, which are still in the country and a part of
its wealth. Our works, therefore, doubly injure us
unless we protect our own industry; first, by letting our enemy, a very viper, into our bosom to
flood us with worthless manufactures; secondly, by
having created this two hundred millions of foreign
debt to sap our resources for ages, and disgrace us
in the bargain.

All the things and circumstances we have been

enumerating show that we have the vantage ground over all the world in respect to manufactures, if we had a sufficiently protective tariff to start them. Our surplus labor, and the active, high, intelligent, moral character of it ; our varied raw materials ; our facility of intercommunication ; our active commerce; our capital ; our water power; coal, iron, wood, lumber, cheap provisions, light taxes, poor laws, and tithes ; climate, savings in freight, profits, commissions, storage, insurances, machinery, inventive genius ; our home-consuming demand or market ; all these and many more prove to us, conclusively, that we do stand on the vantage ground, and have advantages over the whole world, at least as far as our home demand goes.

Other circumstances bear upon this subject, and add still more to our advantages. The public debt of England is eight hundred million pounds, requiring an annual interest of fifty millions ; to which add eight millions poor-rates, ten millions tithes, and twenty millions for an excess of army and navy pension, and civil list expenditures over and above what a moderate government ought to expend ; and it makes a burthen of eighty-eight million taxes annually upon England. This enormous sum may be said to come first out of the profits of labor, before any dividend or enjoyment be had from it. The manufacturers have to pay their proportion of that huge load, which must add to our advantages over her. We have but little national debt, few poor-rates, no tithes, a cheap government, and no excise or taxes that fall particularly on labor. We can use our own raw cotton without even the half-penny duty which it pays going into England, that enhances the price of the raw material that much, and must be greatly felt in the present low price of cotton.

I will here venture a prophecy, that if England by a severe war places another hundred million of debt upon her already overloaded shoulders, she will lose all the markets of the world. We would be foremost in the process, if true to ourselves; for she would be weighed down too low to compete with the active, free, and untaxed American, borne up by all the other advantages that we have enumerated. England dares not engage in another continental war; she knows the consequences.

As a proof and an earnest that we can compete with England and all other countries in manufacturing, if properly protected and started, I would cite the facts and prices growing out of the present condition of our operations in that field. Some articles under the war duties did get a proper start, so as to combine skill and capital both in their operations. I will instance coarse cotton goods, linseys, satinets, glass, paper, shoes and boots, hats, carriages, cabinet and household furniture, plantation cutlery, leather, and a hundred small things of that sort. All these things now go on, to the exclusion of the foreign articles of that kind, up to our consumption, and are made cheaper and of a better quality than we ever had them from abroad.

We have done more than this in these articles, for we are actually shipping off large quantities of them, say eight million dollars worth annually, to all the world, particularly South America, West Indies, Levant, Africa, Calcutta, China, and even have sent some articles to England ; such as cotton drillings, clocks, stamped glass, wooden ware, carriages, and so forth, which have sold to a profit, after encountering her high duties. Our articles are preferred to the English in the other markets where we stand on an equal footing with her. This proves our capacity to manufacture, and it proves also how hard it is to induce capitalists to take hold, and inspire confidence, whilst our policies are so vacillating ; and that they are more afraid of the uncertain legislation on that subject, than of the capacity of our people. What is already stated and proved ought to determine our legislators to establish manufacturing by a proper protection, and give to it stability, so as to inspire confidence.

CHAPTER XIII

PROTECTION IS NOT A TAX ON CONSUMPTION LONG.

WE are told that "protection operates as a tax upon the consumer, is in the nature of a bounty to one class, and a corresponding tax on the other classes of society, and that did it not so operate it would be a mockery, and no inducement or protection at all." This is true but for a short time only. I regard all tariff protection as intended to cover the loss of time necessary to start a new business, and the losses that often occur the first year or two, from the want of skill and experience. By insuring the capitalist that he would be in the end more than compensated for these sort of losses, he is induced to invest his money in machinery and preparations.

So many rush into the business, however, under the inducement, that as soon as a start be made, and skill acquired, competition in this active and enterprising country follows so rapidly, that the prices of the articles made are soon brought down as low as the imported. It is sure to be of a better quality than the foreign, because the manufacturer will not hazard his character and reputation upon which he will depend for life, in making a bad article to be sold and consumed at home. In the supplying of remote markets, dishonesty is often practised in putting up bad or faulty goods. The price and quality of the goods, after competition shall have had its effects, are so low and good that the difference much more than pays back the tax paid for the protection the first few years. This is now verified in the case of such articles as we enumerated in the last chapter, whose difference in price and quality are both vastly in favor of the home production of them. It is becoming true of many others, as fast as skill and experience are combined under an active competition : woollen and iron goods, and a higher class of cottons will soon be in the same situation, and ready to pay us back the costs of protection.   If we pay five or ten per cent. more for two years than we had been in the habit of paying before for goods, and get them two per cent. cheaper for a hundred years thereafter than we previously did, we will be gainers as to price, gainers in the quality, gainers in the steadiness and certainty of the supply, and gainers in the consequent wealth and independence of the country.   Our supply then will be exempt from the hazards of war, the risks of foreign voyages, and the liability to impositions so unscrupulously practised upon strangers.   Our commerce will have the carrying of it, our agriculturists vastly profit by having a home market, and our capital be safely invested.

I would go so far on the principle of protection and bounty as to assert, that there are cases that do arise in most countries, where a government should use money or credit in loaning the means, or giving bounties to enterprising citizens, to enable them to start some branches of business, such as iron and the woollens, that are so necessary to the independence and comfort of all countries. When it is pretty clearly ascertained that these branches would not be developed by individuals, government funds might be used in bounties, in order to insure their production, and the consequent wealth, comfort, and independence, that would be realized from them. For instance, if it were demonstrable that one million would start some lines of business altogether beyond individual means, and that this million would in a few years make two millions, it would follow that it would be a good stroke of policy to do it, and thus develope valuable productions. If the million in those circumstances should make no profit, only secure its eventual return, still it would be good policy to thus use it.

I will now suppose a case where the price of the protected article would be always ten per cent. higher than the foreign one, and still show that it would be sound policy to grant a protection, and the country would be benefited in paying that much more continually for the article. This seems at the first blush a paradox; but on the following hypothesis is proved. Suppose we want ten millions more of goods than we make, and have plenty of idle people, raw material and capital to produce them, but so as to make them worth eleven millions, or one million more than the foreign; the producing of them saves us nine millions, the whole less the advance, nationally speaking, or saves, which would be the same thing, nine millions annually. Our gains would be more than this even, in the rounds, for we enable those idle persons to become consumers and useful, and agriculture is benefited by the home market to that extent, as well as a better condition of things insured. We do not really therefore lose the one million, the seeming difference, much less the nine, because the increased ability imparted, the more active interchanges, the employment of capital, the independence of the nation, the removing the clog to this extent from other occupations, all would be worth infinitely more than this million three times told. This is, however, an extreme case, and can't occur in these United States under our active competition, yet it proves principles. Should the fact be questioned that we do, by our own competition, put the prices down as low or lower than the foreign articles of the same sort, I would verify it by the prices current of the day in England and this country, on such articles as are fully established here, particularly such as are named in the preceding chapter. The sales we are every day making of those goods abroad, alongside of the English, and the preference given to them by the consumers, prove it. When we bring the case home to our own country, the thing works more certainly still, because we always here have a tariff of twenty or thirty per cent. for revenue, which without any regard to the principle of protection is all clear to our manufacturer, and insures success to him after a fair start.

Why should any general law giving protection, or even a bounty, be regarded as partial, and taxing one, even temporarily, for the benefit of another? The law is open to all, and every individual in the community has an equal right to enter the lists and profit by it. If he does not avail himself of it, there is no cause for complaint; it is a proof that he waves his right and gives way to others. Our politicians in this country show a great deal of dishonesty and unfairness in cases like this, and try to pervert and strain facts to make the ignorant believe they are oppressed, that they may make political capital out of it. The idea of monopoly is widely different from this, made of sterner stuff, and intended to favor an individual, or company, at the expense of the community.

We are asked, why keep on the old tariff if the goods become as cheap as the foreign? I answer, that the tariff becomes a dead letter as to fair and honest prices, but is useful as a preventive to the designing. In all countries there are refuse goods, old stocks, unfashionable patterns, and even imperfect goods. These have to be sold, and it is expected at a great loss—but the owners will not sell them at home to affect injuriously their good market, but would send them here, were there no tariff, to be sacrificed, and injure our operations. England, after selling at home, as we have said, one hundred and eighty millions goods, for a good profit, sends off the twenty millions she has left to be sacrificed here. Having her profit already, she cares not for the loss, rather delights in it, from a conviction that she has injured her rival, and possibly prostrated her; for this balance would be enough to ruin us, if thrown annually upon our market. The continuing the duties on, prevents this and keeps the market steady. A country with as much capital as England, with interest worth only two or three per cent., might designedly collect a few millions annually to send goods here, with a view to prostrate our manufactories, and would find her account in it: Say not that this will never occur, when we see now a society existing in England, to get up tariff tracts against protection, and flood this country with them, expressly to change our policy, or prevent our success as a rival. England fears not our sending goods there, for she can prevent that by a tariff; nor would the losing of our market ruin her, because she has other numerous markets; but she foresees that under protection we would manufacture for the world, and take her markets from her.

CHAPTER XIV.

BUYING THINGS OR SPENDING MONEY HOME OR ABROAD IS WIDELY DIFFERENT.

So that a thing is made and supplied at home, it matters but little whether it costs more or less. This is broad ground and needs some illustration, because if true it does away all the objections that can be offered to a protecting tariff. It makes all the difference to the country, taking in its rounds and interchanges of labor, and its capital, whether a dollar is laid out at home or abroad, in buying an article. When it goes to a foreign country to buy the thing, it is gone forever, and becomes the capital or the dollar of that country, after it makes one operation only. Whereas if you lay out that dollar at home, in the neighborhood, or next village, or next state, or district, for an article, it remains in the country, and is still a part of the capital of the country. It does infinitely more than that, because it circulates and repeats its operation of buying an article perhaps one hundred times, possibly a thousand times, and in its rounds serves the purposes of a hundred or a thousand dollars, as the case may be. In the grand rounds of its circulation, it touches as many springs of industry as it does hands, and is all the time doing good. When it shall have done all this, or while it is doing all this, for the thing never ends, it is still a dollar, and counted properly among the dollars or the capital of the country. Figures can't calculate the difference, therefore, in expending a dollar at home or abroad; even the geometrical ratio can't accumulate fast enough to realize this difference. It outstrips every thing but the human imagination in its progress. This vast difference has never occurred to our wisest politicians, much less our demagogues. Now if the article should cost ten per cent. more than the foreign, it is ten times made up in this grand rounds we have alluded to, by the rapid repetition of the thing. It is again made up in the way that prices tally or adapt themselves to one another. If the seller of the article gets a little more, he in his turn pays a little more to the laborers, and they a little more to the farmers, they a little more to the hands, and so on all around the circle, until a perfect equilibrium is not only restored, but kept up between all, and all prices quadrate into a perfect system, that in the rounds can't make the least difference as to the cost or difference of price. I would go so far as to allege and boldly say, that if a country bought all at home, and had nothing to do with foreign markets, it would make no difference to it in the aggregate, or nationally speaking, what an article costs in reason. It would neither add to or impair her wealth or resources. The above point of view is worth much to political economy, and, if understood, would do away the slang and every day arguments of "Tax not one portion of the people for the benefit of the others." It does not operate so at all, even when a difference does seem apparent. On the other principle too the argument fails, as we have seen in a former chapter; that is to say in the operation of skill and competition upon prices, when they shall have had time to act. On both the above principles then there can be no danger, no loss nor tax in a protecting tariff. The country is sure to retain its capital, and have the price reasonable too, or so graduated as not to be felt.

A part of the same argument is the slang expression of "buying where we can the cheapest."

This argument never looks beyond its nose, never once calculates the general effect of things, or takes in the resources, labor, independence, or capital of a country. It overlooks all those sacred duties that would go to give employment to all laborers, develope and bring into action new resources within reach, and save to a nation its capital or income, instead of wasting it in expenditures abroad. It is time the real worth of each and every argument was known and inquired into, so as to not take it as the pass-word of party, or of some district of country that did not understand its own interests, much less those of the whole nation. Our politicians do not realize the great and mighty difference in the result, where all work or only a part of the population. In this case, mathematics can scarcely keep up with results in its ordinary calculations. Suppose, for instance, that one-half of the laborers of a country meet the home supply in manufactures, agriculture, or any other department, and the other half idle; and suppose, too, a market for what all could produce. The country is on a balance and not advancing, this half merely meeting its own home supply, amounting say to one hundred millions worth. Now if the other half goes to work, or is induced to labor and make another hundred million, which finds a market abroad, would not this be a great, clear, and ample income, and enable that nation to save a hundred millions, and add it to its capital? It is clear it would;

and this sort of summing up shows the difference, according to a scale, where all or only a part work or produce.

No nation, no politicians or political economists ought to be content, as long as they see one idle person, whose circumstances require him to labor. All possible stimuli and inducements ought to be applied to rouse his ambition, and show him his interests and worth in the scale of productiveness. Two sorts of arguments take up mankind in relation to the the tariff question. The one, this sort of slang demagogical pass-word of party, calculated to catch the ear of the ignorant, and implant prejudices and impulses in their minds; and the arguments that examine the real and true worth and bearing, in every aspect and shape in which the thing presents itself. The true statesman does this, but is too often met and defeated by the other class, backed by the ignorant, and too often, without their knowing it, by foreign interest. England has put these popular arguments into the mouths of our demagogues, and smiles at the manner in which the gudgeons take and serve her interest. Generally speaking, our tariff laws could not have served our rivals better, if they had penned them themselves, and presided in our councils and legislative assemblies. The English are too wise to attempt any thing through the Federal party, for there they would certainly have failed and alarmed the interests of this country. They chose rather to work through that party that hates England; and seeing that they caught at these slang arguments, and made them popular by repeating them to the people, they rung them in all their changes, until they have almost ruined this country and its best interests. Even results and practical proofs have to give way to these popular notions, that become so obstinate and deep-rooted, that the very facts are either not admitted, or strained into some other channel, and ascribed to causes that are really foreign to them, and had no agency in bringing them about.

One portion of the world is continually sapping and impoverishing another, on the principle at the head of this chapter. England, Germany, and America, expend all of two hundred million dollars a year, by the best estimates, in France, particularly Paris; which sum is gone from those countries for ever, and constitutes the best resource of France. Other nations expend in Italy not less than one hundred million dollars a year, which is the principal income of that country. Hindoostan and Ireland are sapped dry by England, and their very heart's blood flows into London, and swells that overgrown metropolis. This is not only true of distinct countries, but parts of the same country. As soon as any point offers all possible inducements to pleasure and comfort, it becomes absorbing in its character, and drinks up all around it. London, Paris, Vienna, St. Petersburgh, Berlin, Rome, New-York, and many other points, draw all the resources for hundreds of miles around into their vortices, and appropriate them. If this be true of the ordinary expenditures regarding pleasures, enjoyments, and show, it is a hundred times more true of the great purchases and supply of manufactures and the arts. If the population be near enough to these absorbing points to have a daily market offered to them for provision supplies, they reciprocate more immediately with them, and get back as much as they expend; but when a person lives more remote, and gathers up his money by rents or tradings with his neighbors, to expend away from them, it is felt; and the process is impoverishing, because it has no remead or reciprocation in it. We almost dread to see a large fortune spring up in this country, for it is sure to go off to France or England to be expended. If the person who made it by long savings in business does not go, his thoughtless heirs will. We are at work for Europe in more ways than one; we not only pay her our last cent for her manufactures, but lose our capital in this way; and will never scarcely accumulate enough for any great national purpose.

The prices of things, not only in manufactures but agriculture, are not governed, as old writers say, and regulated by the cost of production, or the quantity of labor necessary to make them or produce them, but by the demand for them. All the vibrations in the markets, the ups and downs of prices, are pretty much the result of a greater or less demand for the productions in question among the consumers. An overdone or clogged market is always a bad one; and prices fall in consequence thereof. It is not the product of an acre, for instance, nor the cost of preparing it for cultivation, that constitutes the price of it, but the quantity of land in the market, and the demand for it. Land in England is worth five hundred dollars an acre, and in this country only one and a quarter to ten dollars. Corn or wheat, rather, is worth in England two to three dollars a bushel—here only ninety cents. The same thing is true of all things; they rise or fall, or remain stationary, accordingly as the market or the demand warrants. The only governing quality as to wages is, that the laborer must have enough to subsist upon, or his operation ceases. Within that limit, however, he will often work on, without any other result, for his lifetime. His skill and habits are all shaped to that occupation, or the production of that article; and he holds on, sinks or rises with the price of it, rather than change his habits and pursuit. No part of labor, then, can be said to govern or regulate the price of production, but that part relating to subsistence—all the remaining parts give way to the market or demand, and are dependent on circumstances. Labor may be the foundation of all productive wealth; and yet not be able to govern the prices of articles. It, like the unconscious parent, begets the offspring, but cannot foresee its value and fix its sterling worth. Labor is destined to stand on the lowest level of values, and struggle for bare support, because by the aid of machinery it can overdo all productions, glut all markets, and bring down the prices to this level.

It is a gloomy idea, and presents a sad picture, that in the run of things man is destined to sell himself for bread and clothes, and perhaps brown bread and rags at that. All that political economy can do is to keep up the platform of labor to its greatest productive availability, by giving the best market within its reach, and the best employment to it; and if destined to sink, contrive that all shall keep together, and carry as much comfort with them as possible.

The strongest case in illustration of the above principle, that nations who buy their supplies from abroad never accumulate capital, and all the time remain poor, is found in the history of these United States. We have had a valuable agricultural product all the time, including our staples, and have annually expended it abroad, in buying such things as we should have made at home, and have saved but little capital; because it took our whole ability to supply ourselves with necessaries and luxuries from abroad, which are consumed, leaving not a wreck behind. Our effort has been to make the two ends of the year meet, and prevent balances against us. Have we done this? The worst is to come; and when our present circumstances speak, will show a sad case of debt and thraldom, worse than the spendthrift, who, after using up his income finds himself in the hands of the Jews and usurers. England, after finding that we had not only spent our income with her, and anticipated it by one or two years, and that we had gotten into such an extravagant way as to want more—ten times more, if we could get it, met this want up to all the available credit that we had after our means were exhausted. The evil did not stop there. She agreed to take, and required us to transfer, all the stocks that were available, and promised some dividend to her, including our national, state, corporation, and the one thousand banks that we had started. When all this was done, and the dividends gone from us for ever, as well as the principal, and we still wanted more! cried aloud for more! must have more! the plan was then hit on to call up the states, these sovereignties that stood behind the crowd, and urge them on to useless and empty consumption, and get them to borrow millions under the semblance that they could expend them in developing the country. These sovereignties, urged by demagogues who knew that they would have the handling of the money, came forward and put their sign manual to loans amounting to two hundred million dollars, and issued with much parade bonds and stock to that amount, bearing on an average six per cent. payable semi-annually, or quarterly even, in England, if required. This money reached this country principally in the shape of trashy goods, at two prices, and such things as we either did not need or ought to have made at home, but which we consumed and sunk for ever. That two hundred million gave us that much more ability to buy and consume English goods, which she very well knew, and every cent of it returned rapidly to Europe, principally to England, sure enough, after more goods. So rapidly did it hurry back, that it made no improvements in the country in the shape of cities, farms, schools, and substantial comforts; merely half dug out some canals and ways for roads, and built some board shantees in which to sell liquors and English goods to the laborers, who pretended to be making great works.

What are the facts now? We wake up to debts enough to weigh down our industry for the next fifty years. The states owe in their sovereign capacity two hundred millions; half of it not even paying interest from sheer inability, ten millions of it repudiated, and disgracing in both cases our free institutions and nation. Of bank and corporation and national stocks, besides, two hundred millions held in England, and the individual indebtedness, amounting abroad to fifty millions, making in all the enormous sum of four hundred and fifty million dollars owed abroad, and for what? such things as we might and ought to have made at home. Half of the works aimed at are not finished; such as are completed subserve Europe perhaps nearly as much as ourselves, by letting her into the very bosom of our country, to poison and corrupt still more our very principle of action. We are now paying to England in the shape of interest and dividends not less than fifteen million dollars annually, which will keep us poor for an age to come. The expending, or rather paying for it, is now not even an outlay; fifteen million dollars abroad hurts us

worse, prostrates us more, than paying to one another one hundred millions would; for then the
money is still in the country, and a part of our capital; in the other case it is gone for ever.

There is no calculating such differences; they
appal when run out into their detail. I would lay it
down, then, as a plain principle, and a case proved,
that a nation that supplies itself with articles of necessity or even luxury from abroad, will never accumulate capital or get rich, can only hope to meet
the balance annually. I will further assert, and
appeal to experience in support of the fact, that
they do not meet their balances, but are invariably
in debt abroad. I will also assert, and prove it,
too, that all increase of capital, all issue of stocks,
or loans made by a nation thus circumstanced, is
death to her; for all this, too, travels abroad for
goods. I will finally assert, that these operations
indefinitely postpone the time when such nation will
supply itself, and give to it so much discredit and
such innumerable bad habits and factitious wants,
that she can scarcely ever be available for practical
and economical purposes, and stands mortgaged
and bound for ages to her successful and laughing
masters and rivals.

CHAPTER XV.

HOME MARKET—ITS EXTENT.

LET us estimate the home market, and its extent. I would first lay it down as a sort of axiom, or at least a very sound principle, that all nations ought to make their own supply; not only of provisions but manufactured articles. The home market ought to be secured in an absolute and certain way to their own citizens. In regard to provisions this country has all the time supplied itself. All the Indian corn; all the fruit and horticulture; and fowls, and butter, and other small cultures, such as potatoes, oats, barley, rye, buckwheat, wool, are not only cultivated for the home market, but all consumed by it. Three-fourths of our pork and lard; nine-tenths of our beef; three-fourths of our fish; four-fifths of our flour, say four million barrels out of five, and four-fifths of our lumber are consumed and wanted at home; not counting in this consumption the people who grow and produce these things. So of provisions, of fish, of lumber, we make all, import none, send abroad a good deal, and have therefore the home market complete. We may say the same thing of live stock, ships and commerce, and of the great staples, such as tobacco, cotton, hemp, flax, and others ; some of which, after supplying the home market, leave most of their bulk for export, and are a vast source of wealth to the nation.

It remains to secure the home market for the manufactures ; a very important department of industry, and one that needs it more as an encouragement than all the others. All people must supply the bulk of what they produce as a thing of necessity; for I lay it down as a fixed and certain rule, that no people or nation ever did or can buy all they consume of manufactured articles. They have not the ability to do it ; for their exports, which must come from agriculture, or fisheries, or forests, or mines, constitute the ability. No nation sells enough, therefore, or could sell enough to buy all the fabrics she wants, supposing she made none. We know what our export or ability is ; we know what the ability is of each nation of Europe, and can calculate it very easily. It is a curious fact in political economy, and makes a very curious problem, which should point to and direct politicians in all their tariffs.

By the census and other documents, this nation consumes twelve hundred millions of fabrics or manufactured articles, and imports only sixty millions ; as custom-house data prove. Our ability to import is only ninety millions, and forty of that importation consists of sugar, coffee, tea, wines, and other supplies, that hardly rank as manufactures, and are not counted as such in this estimate. The above assertion sounds strange, and requires some proofs and explanation. That we import but sixty millions of fabrics is proved clearly enough; that our ability to import and consume is a fact of public authority; that we consume twelve hundred millions a year, I will prove by giving a few items that serve as data, in aid of the census, which is never very correct in these side estimates. We are now eighteen millions of population. Take the first great class of supplies, say textures; counting cotton, woollen, silk, hemp, flax, and including not only clothing, but bedding, curtains, and carpets; and putting the consumption on the average at twenty-five dollars a head, it amounts to four hundred and forty millions a year—

	$440,000,000
Hats at $5; shoes and boots at $10 a head, . .	270,000,000
Saddles, harness, bridles, whips, and thongs, $5, . .	90,000,000
Cabinet furniture, including household, $10, . .	180,000,000
Wagons, carts, wheels, carriages, barrows, $10, .	180,000,000
Tools for mechanics, mill-irons, plantation cutlery, $10,	180,000,000
Machinery, steam engines, and all relating thereto, $5,	90,000,000
Iron, nails, castings, stoves, $10, ...	180,000,000
Crockery, kitchen tools, knives, forks, spoons, &c., $10,	180,000,000
Books, journals, newspapers, advertisements, $5, .	90,000,000
Medicines, chemicals, dyestuffs, salts, $10, . . .	180,000,000
Glass, paper, leather, soap, candles, $10, . . .	180,000,000
All other things, $5, ...	90,000,000
	$2320,000,000

Now suppose the above grand total be somewhat overrated, it will certainly leave at least twelve hundred millions for our consumption annually. If we had to buy this from abroad, instead of barter-ing for it in a manner at home, how would we pay for it? We know ninety millions at most is our ability, and after that is exhausted, we would have to go naked or suffer, if we did not make the things ourselves. We are so familiar with the daily house-hold manufactures going on every where, and the daily exchangings based upon them, that they do not excite any interest, and we cease to appreciate them. They are not the less real and invaluable for that reason. England, by the estimate of her writers, consumes even more to the head than we do; say, however, that she consumes twelve hun-dred million dollars worth annually, where could she find the ability to buy all this, since her exports, leaving out her manufactures, amount to nothing, scarcely worth estimating? She is a striking ex-ample, or an extreme case, and would literally go naked and starve, did she not make all at home.

The above estimates and reasonings show the great importance of the home market. We may add here, that we are now spinning up near four hun-dred thousand bales of cotton, one-fifth of the whole production, and the wool of forty million sheep. We use up all the skins and hides we strip; all the sugar we make, say one hundred thousand hogs-heads weighing one thousand pounds each; nearly three million tons of coal, counting bituminous and anthracite; five million bushels of salt; fifty thou-sand tons of iron; all these of our own making, and then import vast quantities of these things besides. We sell to other than the producers at home, four million barrels of flour, and, as we said, other things in proportion. All these goods that we make ourselves are not only cheaper, but of a better quality than the imported, and better serve the population. There is also steadiness in a home market, more especially when we have the raw material too. It cannot be affected by war, nor blockade, nor such like obstructions. Fairness takes the place of knavery, confidence of suspicion, and the nation feels comfortable, rich, and independent. But little money will be wanted to conduct such a home interchange. No foreign exchange in the money market is necessary in connection with it; no drains upon our banks, because there being no pressure, they do not call in or curtail. Every moral principle is cherished, and every interest supported without violating any faith or contracts, and all is mutual and confidential. It is bad enough to depend on foreign countries for luxuries, or such things as our country cannot produce; but wo to that nation that buys its necessaries abroad! She can be affected in her comforts, and even in her very independence, and is virtually tributary. Every branch of business is subserved by having a home market for our manufactures and raw materials, as well as provisions.

I am told here, that since we come so near supplying ourselves even in mannfactures, it is hardly worth any very special laws about it; that the fifty or sixty millions only out of twelve hundred millions that remain to be supplied, will take care of themselves, and in a few years more cover the whole ground. I reply, that some of the things remaining unfurnished at home are articles of necessity, and important to our very independence; such as iron, steel, salt, sugar, crockery, and china, and the finer cutlery; for the want of all which we might suffer on an emergency, and all of which could be made at home. We do not furnish all the flannels, blankets, carpeting, and cloths that we want. A little protection would bring in silks, fine linens, all the fine prints, balzarines, berages, merinoes, cashmeres, double mulled muslins, and all other things that we now depend on foreign countries for. To save sixty million dollars a year, which is tantamount to making it, would enrich this nation very fast, and leave us a completely comfortable people.

The portion of these things that appertain to luxuries, are almost as important to a refined and civilized people, in these times of taste and elegance, as the necessaries. It sets off a people, and gratifies them, when they feel that they can produce such fancy and splendid things, very much. All people must look at home first, (even charity begins there,) and stop not short of securing the home market in its fullest extent to themselves, and stimulating every branch of business up to that point. The home market is like an inherited patrimony; we may claim it as belonging to us, as of right ours. What foreign nation is there that has claims on us for this precious boon, the home market? As well might some rake lay claim to the virginity of some dear ward, and expect us to aid in the prostitution, as to count on enjoying this innate and important privilege of supplying our home consumption.

CHAPTER XVI.

OBJECTIONS ANSWERED TO A PROTECTING TARIFF.

Objection 1st—*No Revenue.* We are asked what we will do for a revenue if we make all our supplies at home? They say there will be no imposts if we import nothing. Our government can collect imposts enough from articles that can't be made or grown in this country; say on tea, coffee, tropical productions, cocoa, chocolate, preserved fruits, West India staples, and such things, for its moderate wants. Its public lands would come in aid; and if all did not do, tax on the ad valorem principle, all values, and licenses. These taxes would be so light as not to oppress or affect the country. It would be years too before all these supplies were made, and the whole ground covered; and in the mean time the high protecting duties would yield revenue enough, with the aid of the public lands, and the articles that we

could not produce. Again, the increased wealth
arising from all this saving and producing, which
would flow in as specie when we fully meet our
home supply, would well bear taxation, and could
afford to keep up the revenue of so just and paternal a government.

Objection 2d—Have wild or back Lands. We
are told that we have fertile back lands in abundance, and our surplus population can occupy
them, and be comfortable and independent if
not rich. This is that fixed hog and hominy
state, or rather the log cabin state, which means,
raise meat and bread and eat them, and wear
homespun. In this age of improvement, why stagnate and barbarize the human family, by casting
them in the woods remote from all comfort and
civilization ? Overdone as agriculture is, they could
not hope to make any money or any thing to sell.
I have known new settlements, remote from all navigation and the interchanges of commerce, to remain stationary for twenty years in this log cabin
state. No change during all that time except some
dirt, smoke, and dilapidation gathering around the
cabin. The individual begins by building a cabin
worth ten dollars, clears a few acres of land, has a
sow and pigs, a cow and calf, and a horse, and one
or at most two beds on ash stands. He has some
corn and pork, and hunts a little. His wife spins,
and by hand makes some linsey or cotton goods of
the coarsest sort, with which to clothe all including herself. They are able to buy nothing out of

the farm but a little salt and iron. No education for the children, or books, newspapers, society, or churches, for themselves. All is rough, selfish, and barbarous; and the head of the cabin, nothing but a corn-growing Indian. All advance in taste, luxury, and information, is precluded. Is this a desirable state in this age of light and improvement? Does it contribute any thing to the credit, prosperity, or resources of the nation? This is agriculture on new lands, in the back woods; we want no more of it, we have had a surfeit. The human mind must advance in this age; it can't even be stagnant without going backwards relatively. In this young country, where a thousand things can be done if the government be true to its own interests, and give the proper inducement, all ought to be put in train to advance, and be so placed as to obey the impulses of gain and independence. When we see a young people thrown out of profitable employment, we may take it for granted that something is wrong, that the governors of the country do not promote its interests, and insure its prosperity and developement. The body of the people seem to understand the rough and unpropitious state of a back-woods settlement, and will almost suffer rather than encounter it. They are willing to go to any sort of manufacturing or commercial pursuits, rather than into the woods. The backs lands are a resource to the country, and will do in the last resort, but then only.

Objection 3d. We are told that commerce

will suffer and stagnate if we make all of our own
supplies, that there will be nothing for it to occupy
itself with. The answer to this is very simple.
Commerce, as far as relates to buying and selling
on the wholesale or retail principle, will be as well
or better occupied, and taken up with domestic
commerce, and interchanges, than with foreign.
They are more bulky, and safer, and the whole
operation more steady. No wars to jeopardize, or
blockades to obstruct, or ups and downs of currency from overtrading and reaction. All moves
steadily and safely and profitably on to support
and respectability, if not wealth. A merchant
at home has confidence in his own business; he
sees in it a certainty of support; and his mind
is not harassed all the time with anxiety for the
future fate of his capital and his family. Hence
he is not on the everlasting stretch to make a large
fortune soon, or to prevent the loss of one, and is
therefore a better citizen, and safer subject. As
to foreign commerce, what will be left of it, will be
pretty much as it now is. Tonnage will be taken up
in carrying our bulky raw materials and provisions
abroad, and bringing back such things as we do
not raise or make. I see nothing to affect commerce unfavorably in the case, but some things,
and much to stand it on a better and safer footing,
and render it a more steady and regular occupation.
In my chapter on commerce, I will show that our
tonnage duties as to foreign intercourse want regulating, and to be put on a more just footing for our

interests. I shall defer my ideas on commerce as a national policy, until I shall have finished my remarks on manufactures.

Objection 4*th*. Another objection to this course is, they say, "that if we import no manufactured goods, the balance of trade will be too much and too continually in our favor, and Europe will have to send specie to meet this balance." "That too much specie will flow here, enough to impair the quantity in Europe, producing spasms there, in the banks of England and France particularly, and deranging all their values, exchanges, and currency." "The consequence will be positive laws prohibitory of the exportation of specie, and very probably a revolution in England." "That the prices and values of things will be greatly affected there; so much that a little money will buy a great deal, and those nations be unable to take our raw materials at all." It is further said, " that the abundance of money here will lead to extravagance and idleness, and make every thing worth so much money, produce as well as manufactures, that there will be no standard between us and Europe, by which to regulate values." They say too that " the price of our surplus raw materials will be so low, that those great staple districts will suffer much relative loss." Finally, "they predict so general and wide-spread derangement of business and values, that the whole world will be put out of her ordinary routine of business, and have to seek new connections." All this is too vivid a picture, and one that will not be realized to the extent of much mischief and derangement. Values will be somewhat affected, but not so much as to produce spasm. All our difficulties here will be compensated by the great abundance of money, which we can use in the arts and in plate. And all the difficulties in Europe yield to the fact, that less money will buy all they want, and serve them just as well as more did. Some new channel, some new device, or new productions and barters, will come in aid of such a state of things, and restore the balance. The growers of the raw materials in our country will be mainly supported by our own demand, which, under a proper protection, will become the absorbing one, and govern the market. Should we get under way, aided by a protecting tariff, we will not stop short of supplying the whole world, and taking, with our advantages, all the markets under our control and management.

Objection 5*th.* We are told "that if a tariff be laid strong enough to protect and encourage the making of the whole supply, that smuggling will spring up and impair or defeat the whole object aimed at." This has been the standing cry of all the anti-tariff party from time immemorial, but their prophecies have not been fulfilled to much extent. The hazards of smuggling amount to a pretty large protection, and by the time they are paid, and something for the wear and tear of character and conscience allowed for, there will not be much smuggling. Our own competition, too, springs up so rapidly, that prices are soon so nearly balanced here and in England that there is no margin left for smuggling. This bugbear, clothed in immorality, and without any patriotic feeling about it, ought not to deter the real friends of their country from doing their duty. As well might a national legislature refuse to pass a law against any crime, because some member alleged that some rascals would escape the penalty of the law. The Atlantic ocean is so wide, and our revenue police and cutters so active, that but few will attempt it.

Objection 6th. Another objection to manufacturing very extensively is, "that it confines the operatives and their families so much that they become immoral, unhealthy, and the race degenerates." There are such scenes in England, where wages are small and cut down to minimum rates, or bare subsistence. In this country, as far as we have yet gone, comfort, health, decency, and education accompany that class; and they are as intelligent, healthy, and moral, as any portion of our population that has to labor. The manufacturing operations can be carried on consistently with all that is due to a useful population. All the pride of patriotism, decency of person, neatness of dress, purity of manners and language, comport with that state in this country. A population thus concentrated, and decent and orderly, can be made very scientific by night lectures, and libraries. The Lancastrian monitorial system of education can be applied to the rising generation, and night lectures and experiments take up the adults. In New England an *esprit de corps* for decency, morality, religion, and character, runs with the operatives, that has done wonders, and preserved sobriety, temperance, and self-respect, as well as morality, virtue and industry. In New England, a great deal of money is not only made, but saved, and invested in savings banks for future use.

Where thousands of young women are collected about the factories of Lowell, Nashua, Great Falls, Pawtucket, Patterson, and other places, there is scarcely an instance of bastardy; not so many they say, who know, as among the same amount of farmers, or agriculturists. Ideas become property in common among them. The health of the manufacturers of New England is not worse, nor even as delicate as the people in cities, particularly in those parts of cities where the poor live, generally in confined and dirty lanes. Nothing need be jeopardized, then, on the score of health or morals, in the case of the operatives in the manufacturing districts of this country, taking the facts named above as data and the basis of all new establishments; and much may be gained in comfort, taste, and education, over agriculturists, from this favorable situation.

Objection 7th. It is contended and used as an objection to the protecting tariff, " that if we make our own supplies up to the full, Europe, and England in particular, would not take our raw materials." They pretend that she does that on the principles of reciprocal trade, and takes our raw things, as far as we take her goods. This is not true; for they take no more of our things, at any rate, than they want, and must have. The idea of mutual interest never entered into their calculations. They shut their ports against our provisions and corn, and against all of our manufactures, by such high duties, that none scarcely go in, and yet clamor if we attempt to supply our own wants. This is reciprocity with a vengeance. History could not furnish an instance of more selfishness than England manifests, or more arrogating injustice. We have the meanness too of not only not countervailing it, but actually contributing to keep up that one-sided state of trade. Our anti-tariff politicians, are as much playing into the hands of the English, in all their measures, as if the words were put into their mouths by England, and our laws penned by her too. It is strangely inconsistent that a party should exist in this free country, in one breath abusing England with fixed hatred, and in the next moment contributing to all her injustice, and even preferring her interests to New England, as to manufactures. I have witnessed cases where English goods of a worse quality, and dearer, were preferred to better goods from New England. England goes on the principle of buying nothing but raw materials, or such tropical or southern luxuries as she can't produce, and buys them invariably where she can the cheapest.

No nation has acted more impolitically, with

all her shrewdness and selfishness, than England.
She has, by her injustice, and grasping arrogance
and war, forced the United States into manufacturing, pretty well up to their own consumption.
Nothing of the sort was aimed at before England
began her oppressions. Had England had foresight enough to have made with us reciprocal
treaties, based on mutual interests and on our respec-
tive productions, both nations would have found
their interest in it. Had England, for instance, let
our corn and pork in at a low, or no duty, and our
raw materials too, we would have leaned on agriculture with a view of supplying her, and never
have gone into manufactures, except in the family
way. On the lowest estimate, if England had
taken our corn, and provisions generally, since the
year 1790, it would have counted us by this time
one thousand million of dollars, at the least, and
have enriched us. She too, would have secured in
us an everlasting customer, that would of course
have enriched her in a still more signal way; for
manufacturers in interchanges always, from the
nature of the productious, have advantages over
agriculturists. Nothing but her aristocracy and
a short-sighted policy, has held her to the restrictive system in regard to us and our provisions.
Her loss is irreparable, for she has lost her best
customer for ever, and built up for herself a rival in
all the markets of the world besides. No two nations ever existed, that could have played into each
other's hands so completely, as this country and

England; from the diversified character of their productions, and capacities to furnish such things as each wanted. This was seemingly aided too by the same language and habits, free institutions, and enterprise in their people.

Let us now go back to the first idea, " that England will not take our raw materials unless we take her manufactures;" analyze it a little closer, and look at it in its true bearings. Is it not surprising, and past all belief, that our greatest men from the south, and many of the leaders of party, should have risked their reputation for thought, and character, and consistency, so far as to have asserted, on the floor of Congress, " that unless we take our supplies of goods from England, she will not take our raw cotton?" And further, " That because the export of cotton gives us most of our export value, it must pay and does pay one-half of all the imposts?" " That the growers of it do to that extent," they say, " pay the taxes of this government." This last idea is too absurd for serious discussion, and can't hope to disturb the self-evident fact, that it is the consumer, the world over, that pays the tax. We leave that to its own absurdity, and inquire into the other idea, " that England will not take our raw material, of cotton particularly, unless we take our supply of goods from her." England has been true all the time to her maxim of buying what raw materials she wants, wherever she can buy the cheapest, and in no instance does she depart from it. I will lay it down as a fact, tha

all our cotton, as well as what is made every where
else, is wanted and actually consumed.   The stock
even now in England, although comparatively
large, is fading away so fast as to almost create an
alarm.   We will illustrate this subject now, by a
fact that will perhaps produce some surprise.   We
send to Europe about 1,700,000 bales of cotton
now, and take back in the shape of cotton goods
of all sorts, from every nation, only 60,000 bales
in all.   I prove this in this way: our custom-house
furnishes the data that we are now importing
but 8,000,000 dollars worth of cotton goods from
the whole world.   Now by casting our data upon
the difference of the raw and wrought value of
cotton, we can come at the fact.   The wrought
value of such fine goods as we take from Europe,
is six times the raw.   Now if 8,000,000 dollars buy
the wrought, by the inverse rule of three what must
the raw, entering in it as one to five, cost?   The
answer is about 60,000 bales.   This fact would
have astonished those great politicians referred to,
if they had ever extended their minds so far, or if
their prejudices would have suffered it.   Were our
custom, therefore, withdrawn from England, it
would not be felt much.   This fact bears directly
on the idea, that England will not take our cotton
unless we take her goods, and shows its emptiness.
England wants our raw cotton for her other customers and her own consumption, and must have
it.   She is now consuming thirty thousand bales a
week, and must have all of 1,500,000 bales to

make up her quota and prevent her spindles stopping, which would be spasms and death to her in these times of general thrift.

CHAPTER XVII.

OUR CAPACITY TO GROW COTTON CHEAPER THAN ANY COUNTRY.

ANOTHER question arises in connection with the above, as to the capacity to grow cotton in the United States, compared with other nations, and whether the market can be supplied and overdone, or not? The capacity in the United States to grow cotton, hardly knows any limits. I will assert here that we can grow it cheaper than other nations, up to any demand for it, and will take the markets of the world for that article, particularly on this side of the Cape of Good Hope. Slavery is fixed enough in the United States, to count certainly on its productions for the next fifty years at least, and will take hold of the staple of cotton, stronger and stronger every year. The average crop in this country now, is two million bales; of this we spin four hundred thousand. England wants at least, one million bales of *our* cotton, and the balance of Europe, not less than six hundred thousand. We see that our crop is now fully up to the consumption of the whole market, and will increase faster

than that consumption.   It is calculated that with
Texas our annual increase of production will be
not less than two hundred thousand bales, whilst
the increased consumption will not be much more
than half of that amount.   We can grow cotton
cheaper than any other people, and of a better
quality.   As our agriculture is so much overdone in
other productions, and as so many slaves are nearly
idle north of the cotton district, and no limit to the
fertile, cheap land, and a suitable climate for cotton, the tendency is that way, and continual and
great increase may be looked for in its growth.
Nothing is looked to by these slaveholders but
annual surplus, I mean the balance that is in hand
at the end of the year, over and above the outlay
and expenses for that year.   They own the slaves,
and never count them as capital or calculate any
interest on their cost unless a new plantation is being made as an investment by some capitalist;
where the land and slaves have all to be bought,
then the annual profit is calculated.   There are
few new investments in that way; all the increase
of crop is from an increase of slaves, partly in a
natural way, and partly by their owners bringing
them from the north, where they were unproductive.

Let us now calculate what cotton can be grown
for, when prices get down to a mere support for
master and slave.   With the proper economy, by
the owner living on his place, deriving his house-
hold and table expenses from it, and clothing and

feeding his own slaves, his annual expenses, counting salt, iron, medicines, taxes, wrapping for his
cotton, and overseer's wages, do not exceed two
cents a pound on the product or crop ; all over that
is profit in their sense, that is, over and above annual expenses. I will give the detail to make this
clear. A plantation of fifty hands, makes the
average of seven bales to the hand, weighing four
hundred and fifty pounds; this is three hundred
and fifty bales. Suppose two cents for expenses,
this amounts to $3150 on the crop. This crop, say,
sells for four cents a pound neat, and, clear of
charges for transportation, insurance, and commissions for selling, leaves $3150 profit for the luxu-
ries of the owner, who gets his necessaries out of
the plantation by living on it. This is a very
pretty sum ; and half of it would be ample for him,
which would reduce cotton to three cents. As to
insurance, unfortunately the slaves not only insure
themselves, but give a large increase, which grows
up with the owner's children, and furnishes them
with outfits by the time they need them. Now I
will go into a calculation to show that two cents a
pound cover the annual expense. Here follow the
items, taking a plantation of fifty hands as a basis.
—For overseer, $500; for salt, $20; iron, $30;
medicines, $20; doctor's bill, $100, for you can
contract by the year, and it is often done at two
dollars a head ; bagging and rope to wrap it, at
twelve and a half cents for the one, and five cents
for the other, amount to $300; taxes, $100; sun-

dry small things, $100, all told. (The writer speaks
from experience, for he is a planter of cotton and
owns slaves.) All this amounts to $1070, much
below the allowance of two cents a pound, amounting, as we have seen, to $3150. I only wish to
show that we can grow cotton at three cents a
pound, and have a living profit. This will carry
on the culture unabated, and increase the population from the sources named. It is one of those
accumulated tides that rolls itself on; or one
of those sweeping tornadoes that carries on its
might by some inherent elasticity. We can grow
it cheaper than all other people for the above reasons, and take the whole supply of the world, at
least our world, this side of the Cape of Good
Hope. Besides the calculations of cost gone into
above, we know the fact, that as long as there is
any surplus or result annually above expense, the
slaves engaged in it will go on, and with increased
energy and skill, just in proportion to the lowness
of price. This habit the slave-owner has of not
counting his slaves as capital at all, or sinking them
to nothing in the estimate, as far as investments
are concerned, is hard to meet, and still harder to
beat. Were there any other cultures that promised
the certainty of a better and permanent profit to
slaveholders, there would be some danger of having this staple affected. It however is as profitable
as any; less overdone, and more permanent in its
character and market. This, in connection with
the fact that they are in possession of costly ma-

chinery fixed in this culture, will keep all the slaves and their increase at it all the time. There is an energy and skill in the masters of this country that not only organizes slavery in a safe way, but stimulates it, and makes it almost twice as productive as it ever was in the West Indies, or South America. This is more manifest in the cotton culture than others, and powerfully affects its volume and profits. This habit of looking to annual results or surplus only, will insure the continuance of this culture, even in the poorer lands, where, although the profits are less, they show some result; and being on account of the poverty of the soil the more healthy, the owners all live on their property and need less income. The cotton culture then is sure to go on in this country, at any price, from three cents up, that the market warrants, and with increased energies. These facts warrant us in asserting, which we do broadly and unqualifiedly, that we can grow cotton cheaper than any other people on earth, not even excepting the Hindoos. The consequence of this will be that we will take the market of the whole world, and keep it supplied with cotton.

Let us now institute some comparison between the United States and other countries, in reference to this culture. The other country that we dreaded most as a rival is Brazil. Here I will make one general remark, that applies emphatically to America and the West Indies, that is, that no free men ever have or will, at minimum prices, cultivate cotton at all. The only cotton then sent out of this continent, will be grown by slaves. Brazil is a slave country, and a fertile one. The cotton crops have been for many years without much increase, running about two hundred thousand bales of the weight of ours. As cotton falls in its price, does she quit its culture, and go to others. She has the sugar, coffee, cocoa, dyestuffs, diamonds, gold, and all the tropical productions to back upon, when cotton does not promise a profit. Sugar and coffee there are increasing because slavery in Hayti, the British Islands and Caraccas, has been discharged, and sugar and coffee affected to that extent; for as sure as the sun rises, all heavy staples will cease with slavery ere long. Hayti once flooded Europe with her sugar ; now she does not produce enough for her own use. Brazil, therefore, whilst her slavery lasts, will not cultivate cotton at low prices, but lean on her other staples ; at the least she will not increase her cotton culture; and the next revolution there will most probably put an end to slavery, and mix it in with the population, that is pretty well tainted with the blood, and prepared for such an event. Brazil need not then be feared as a cotton-growing rival. Next comes the West Indies, including Berbice, Demarara, and Surinam. In the West Indies, the cheniel, storms, and better staples have banished cotton long since; and it is no longer among their staples. Berbice and Demarara are rather exceptions. The facts, however, there, do not favor any increased culture. In the English part, slavery is discharged, and soon will be in the other parts of that region.   France, Holland, Sweden, and Denmark, will soon discharge slavery in their islands and on the main, and some of the revolutions ere long reach the Spanish islands. We now come to Egypt and the Levant.   In the latter region it amounts to nothing; and in Egypt is a forced culture on the principle of slavery, and will end with the Pasha's life in a few years.   The change, and most probably the distraction attendant on the Pasha's death, will put an end to this organization.   It never exceeded two hundred thousand of our bales, and will be less before it is more.   The Pasha says, moreover, that he will not grow it at the present low prices; as he has his corn, and sugar crops, and even rice, that will be more profitable.

We will now go to the East Indies, Bombay, and other parts of the British possessions in Hindostan.   Much has been said as to the capacity and cheapness of this country, in reference to the cotton product, and many threats thrown out both by the English, and our own politicians, as to what this great country can or would do.   This has led to much inquiry, and I have convinced myself that we can beat even the East Indies in this culture; and will beat them out of all the markets of Europe and, I believe, China.   They have never raised it under four cents as a staple; and will not, because they are an indolent people; have no wants, and cannot be stimulated without great rewards or

inducements.   Labor is cheap there, but very inefficient; one American slave is made to do as much as
five of those laborers, at the safest estimate.   They
have no contrivance, or spirit, or ingenuity.   Their
cotton is of a very low and bad quality, and, from
experiments lately made, cannot be improved.   The
reason is, it rattoons or becomes a tree, and the cotton borne on these trees is short, harsh, small in
quantity, and very difficult to gather.   All rattoon
cotton, even in the West Indies, or South America,
is of a worthless and very inferior quality.   Americans and good machinery were taken out to Bombay to improve the quality of their cotton.   These
men were neighbors of mine, and since their return,
I have seen and talked with them in detail.   They
are practical men, and do not hesitate to say that
the culture there, on the American annual planting
system, is a total failure, and from the nature of the
climate must be so.   The climate is too dry; needs
irrigation, which alone insures a failure.   When
the market is excited enough for orders to go from
Europe to Bombay for cotton, the factors pass the
word, and the Gentoos go to work and collect it
from the trees growing around their huts, or around
waste places, until the quantity wanted is made up.
Then it all ceases until the market authorizes another picking.   This accounts for the ups and downs
of the cotton market in Europe, for the last fifty
years.   As soon as the stock diminished enough in
Liverpool to create any alarm or anxiety about the
supply, up went the price, sometimes to thirty cents.

Then heavy orders went to the East Indies, and the high price stimulated the Gentoos to strip every tree in the whole land to fill these orders, and a large quantity of cotton arrived in Europe, enough to swell the stock and dash the price down to less than half what it was. The same thing was repeated as fast as they worked the stock down; hence the vibrations that we have witnessed in the cotton market; some of them of magnitude enough to disturb all the interests in Europe and America, and produce convulsions in the money market, by deeply affecting all values. Fortunately for the country, and particularly for Europe, these vibrations must now cease; because our crops hereafter, and even now, do meet all the wants of Europe, and furnish a better quality of cotton to the manufacturers. Our crop will never again, as we have shown above, drop below the consumption; on the contrary, will keep ahead of it enough to let down the price to the minimum. Then, as said before, we will have the whole market, and even the Surats no longer travel around the Cape of Good Hope. The markets then of every thing will be more steady, for cotton seems to be the master spirit that disturbs all, and deranges all. The American master will lean upon his low, but certain income; raise all his supplies, and make a thousand improvements that will redound to the comfort of the slaves, and the pride and elegance of the owner. In the cotton culture there is time to do much in the way of improvements. The slaves are many of them car-

penters, masons, smiths, brick-makers, and garden-
ers, and can do all these things between the coming
in of a new crop, and the going out of the last.   A
planter, too, can and does raise all his food, both
meat and bread, and a comfortable supply of vegetables, and a dairy; and does all this without taking
any time from the cotton, for these things are
either incidental cultures, or come in before or after
cotton, so as not at all to interfere with it.   I am
not speaking hypothetically, when I say the United
States can grow all the cotton wanted; have slaves
and land enough to do it, and even overdo it.   This
country can raise three million bales, just as easily
as she now does two millions, when that much is
wanted, and then keep ahead of the consumption
far enough to prevent any advance in the price.
This culture embraces such an extent of country,
from the Roanoke to the Rio Grande on the sea-
coast, turning some very prominent capes, and from
the Cumberland river to the Gulf of Mexico, that
it cannot fail extensively from any one cause.   The
worms prevail in one district, and twenty others
have none.   A drought never affects more than
one-fifth or one-sixth at a time, nor too much wet
either.   A tornado is always very limited; and an
extensive gale never reaches the Atlantic and Gulf
both in its sweepings.   Nothing can therefore prostrate one-fourth of a crop, or even one-fifth of it at
once.   The production is sure to be adequate, and
keep ahead of all wants.

This is a fact upon which, both in England and

in this country, much might be built as regards the great interests of the money operations, manufactures, and commerce. Some of the best and most important principles in political economy might derive aid and illustration from it, and many great movements be governed by it. It behooves all political economists, all financiers, all statesmen, all manufacturers, and merchants, to examine the facts closely before they make any changes in their business. If we keep cotton down, not to its minimum price, but to five or six cents, it will cease to come around the Cape of Good Hope, and the United States have the market of the world just as certainly as at three cents. The Surats are the last rivals that are to be vanquished by the superior energy, ability, and organization of this country, and forced to quit the field that legitimately belongs to us. England and Europe owe us thousands of millions of money for cotton crops yet unborn, but which time will mature, and enable us to close this great mortgage that nature and art have given to us upon the industry of the world. The carding of cotton and wool together will carry the use of cotton into the winters of every country, and increase its consumption one fourth at least. A sort of goods are thus made that fit all warm or temperate latitudes, and the two seasons of the year, fall, and spring, that are too warm for woollen, and too cold for cotton. There is a suppleness in these goods that fits them admirably for ladies' clothing and children's, where the form and action

will not be encumbered. Substitution of cotton
for many things will take place when the value is
let down to a low price, and give greater extent to
its use. Three million bales at four cents a pound,
is eighteen dollars a bale, and will amount to the
enormous sum, even at that minimum price, of
fifty-four million dollars, which will be realized by
one fifth part of the population of the United States,
counting slaves and children, and leaving out the
slaves, by one-tenth part of this nation. This is
fully one half of the revenue of the country arising
from exports. This shows what a margin the cotton interest has yet for profit, and how truly, as we
have said, it can descend much lower in the scale
of compensation to its producers, and enable them
to live comfortably, and carry it on to the same and
greater extent. The whole body of slaves will,
like the northern Goths and Vandals, move south-
wardly in a body, or enough of them to put the profits
of the cotton culture as low as grain and tobacco
have become, and equalize labor of that descrip-
tion in the United States.

The above showing and reasoning does away
the idea with which our own and English politicians threaten us, " that England would not take
our raw cotton if we refused to take her goods;
would draw her supply from other quarters, and
stimulate her own East Indies to produce enough
to meet her demand." She dare not decline taking
our cotton, for it is cheapest, and because she has
built up her manufactories on the minimum price

of the raw material, and buys it wherever cheapest, and have conformed all prices of labor and goods to that principle. England has in France and Germany, as well as in us, rivals to her cotton manufactures, and such skilful rivals, too, that she dare not pay more for the raw material than they do. If she were to pay two cents a pound more for cotton than we do, or than the Continent of Europe does, she would lose her hold on the cotton manufacture, and her opponents would take her markets. The half penny a pound duty now levied in England, will have to give way to insure her success. There is no danger then of England ever paying more for raw materials, by the operation of a law of her own passing, than the rest of the cotton world. For the same reason she cannot afford to give a bounty to the East or West for raw cotton; it would throw her behind, and prostrate her. We have seen that the Surats cannot be grown and brought around the Cape, where double freights exist, as cheap as we can furnish a better article. England will continue, in the nature of things, and from the very necessity of the case, to take our cottons as far as she wants them, and pay for them in specie, even if we should not want her manufactures. Another branch of the argument is, that if we want nothing from England, our crop will not be wanted. We have made this all clear in the previous paragraphs. We will merely add here, that between us and England it is a plus and minus state, as to the consumption of cotton. **What** we spin more, England spins less, and vice versa, which would leave the great principle of demand and supply exactly on the same ground as it was on before. There would be this difference, however, that we spinning one-third or one-half of the crop would create two markets for our cotton, two sets of bidders, and a competition that is always worth something to a market. We would profit by this, and have already profited by it: according to the opinions of our most deserving and most skilful commission merchants and factors, our own spinners are now worth fully two cents a pound to the cotton market each and every year, by the competition they create with the Europeans. Let this competition go further, until all monopolies cease in that great field of demand and supply, and an honest bidding between the consumers goes on regularly. This would be another means of steadying the market, and placing every thing in relation to this great interest on a calm and certain footing. In England the cotton has become the great and absorbing interest of the nation. When any thing happens to this vital principle with her, all becomes paralyzed, and her very constitution seems to give way. All her members sympathize with the spasms which this interruption of the circulation of her very heart's blood produces. In the use of cotton she is like the sot, who, steeped in liquor, tries to live without its stimulus and sinks in the attempt; she must have it, and must spin it, and must sell it, and must live upon it.

Fears have been expressed, that "should we get under way by the stimulus of a protecting tariff, we would not only pass the dead point, but go ahead beyond our own consumption, so as to aim at supplying the whole world with manufactures." "That large towns would spring up and exhibit the scenes of distress that Manchester, Birmingham, Sheffield, and other places in England do, and create a miserable population," which, put upon minimum wages, could save nothing, and be subject, on every reverse of business, to all possible misery. This might be prevented, if taken in time, by laying an export duty on all manufactures leaving this country.   Such arguments cut like two-edged swords, and show how much might be done under a protection.   A cheap clothing would add very much to the comfort and decency of the world, and stand all in an array of becoming respectability, as to appearance, that would inspire in them self-esteem and a consciousness of something capable of taking care of themselves.   In the savage state, and before cotton wrapped mankind, they suffered for clothing, and rags indicated poverty. Now all may be clothed that choose to work one day in the week, and abstain another day from drink and tobacco.   What effect is all this facility destined to have on man?   It will teach him never to despond and sink under his circumstances, no matter how narrow and restricted they may be.

CHAPTER XVIII.

MANUFACTURES WILL HAVE A GOOD EFFECT ON OUR
GENERAL PROSPERITY, AND EACH BRANCH OF BUSINESS.

General Prosperity. Let us now look a little
closer into the effect, that the encouragement of
manufactures would have upon the general prosperity of this country, and upon each branch of
business and separate interest in particular. I
have clearly shown above that we are ripe for
them, and that drawing or diverting labor from
overwrought agriculture, commerce, and our cities,
would do much good, and relieve those cases from
great depression. All occupations or branches of
business would exert more elasticity, and be the
more vigorous and healthy for it. Five hundred
thousand laborers put to work, with all the aids of
machinery, could, according to estimates well established from facts in England, produce two hundred million dollars worth of goods: if we went
up to the consumption of the country only, less
than one half of this sum would produce much
wealth and prosperity, and work wonders upon
this nation. If we went beyond the home supply,

the overplus would be the means of a vast barter or trade with South America, the West Indies, the Levant, and China. We would use the foreign market then as England now does, that is, to vent surplus manufactures upon. Our home market would increase much and rapidly from the increased ability all this would give, and the thousand springs of industry that would be touched by the operation, including its transportations, storages, commissions, agencies, and all concerned in such extended transactions. In a country of such varied interests and articles of both art and agriculture, if things did become overdone, an extensive barter system would take the grand rounds, until a man's labor might be turned into all the comforts and elegancies of life, and through such interchanges present a state without a further want. How different this from the log-cabin state we described above! Our market and prices then would become steady, and to be calculated in reference to any interest. No vibrations, occasioned by wars, short or abundant crops, and speculating rage, that, having their bases in Europe, in overtradings, and wild calculations, prostrate our merchants, drain our specie, destroy credit, and suspend our banks. This state of things tends to drive the fair and regular trader from his business, and leaves the field to the unprincipled and desperate adventurer. If war now assails us, or rages even in Europe, we become involved. Our scattered and floating capital, at the mercy of tyrants and revolutions, may be seized or compromited, as we have more than once seen it, and, what is worse now, we have no home market to back upon. We have seen this fair country suffering for the want of the commonest articles of necessity in a war, and forced to get them from the very enemy we were fighting, by illegal licenses. In the last war with England, we had not iron, salt, blankets, flannels, and woollen goods enough for necessity, much less comfort. A nation becomes independent in making or producing such things. We hesitate now to fight or go to war for our most sacred rights, lest we suffer privations and discomfit. In place of all these effects and privations, we would have a prosperity that would in its tide embrace all interests by encouraging and protecting manufactures. An unsteady market and an uncertain state of things are very demoralizing to all nations. In a single season a people often lose half their capital, particularly the mercantile and trading portion thereof. Losses of this kind run in a sad train. Overtrading at home leaves debts abroad unpaid and credit ruined, exchanges against us, specie leaving the vaults of our banks, and they, to sustain themselves, have to curtail, and the whole mass of the people become then affected. The commerce of the country becomes crimped down to nothing, prices of produce and all values nominal, merchants grow desperate, conceal, lie, swindle, first their creditors, then the government. These things work on, un-

til the whole trade, commerce, and capital of the
country is swept off, and all get into the hands of
foreigners, who have no interest to restore things.
This overtrading, which is generally the root of
this evil, would not exist if we were making our
supplies, instead of reaching out in this way after
them, and involving all in speculation and uncertainty. Instead of all this confusion, immorality,
and loss, give me the home market and a manufacturing interest to supply it, and let me enjoy all the
prosperity appertaining to it. This would be a
general prosperity and thrift, the accumulation of
wealth and capital, the increase of comforts and
elegancies, and even luxuries, and the reality as
well as the feeling of independence.

Agriculture. Let us now show the bearing and
influence a tariff would have on all the productions,
all the staples, all the occupations, the interests, the
capital, and character of the country and its citizens.
I will consider, first, the effect of a protecting tariff
on our agriculture, the very foundation of our subsistence and wealth. When the agriculturists and
manufacturers, the producers and consumers are
brought together, it is better ; much time is then
saved in serving them, and much capital in transportations. Many of the small cultures that make
a show on the stalls of a market, and contribute
much to comfort and support, will not bear to be
carried or transported far. They must be consumed near the place where they are raised. When
a factory is situated in the very midst of such small

cultures, a beautiful series of exchanges or barter goes on, and the laborers have all these sorts of supplies right at their doors, to be paid for in their goods. There is more profit in these small things, such as garden vegetables, dairies, chickens, eggs, pigs, lambs, green corn, and the like; and at the same time they are more healthy and acceptable to the operatives, carried fresh, as they would be, for their use. Around the large cities and in other places the lands are in small lots, and suit this sort of culture, whilst the heavy grain products lie further back. The small operations in agriculture take up the weaker hands, whose labor in such things is as productive as stronger labor on the grain and pork farms. We see in New England, where many manufacturing establishments are in successful operation, the stimulating effects thereof upon agriculture. The fields are brushed up and manured, cleared of stones and briers, and in a state of high productiveness, exactly in proportion as they are nearer to or farther from some manufacturing village or consuming population, or a people able to purchase them. In other parts of that country, where there is no water-power or facilities to induce such establishments, we see agriculture neglected; the farms look exhausted, and the fences and improvements dilapidating, the stones, briers, and jungle prevail, except in some corner naturally fertile, where the owner cultivates a little for his own use. You may tell, therefore, by the state of the agriculture, when you approach or re-

cede from these manufacturing points. When remote, the husbandmen are off, trading on their wits,
or fishing to gain a little money, which a neglected
farm denies to them. A population consumes, even
of provisions, according to its ability; if poor and
without money to purchase, or valuable products to
barter, they crimp, and pinch, and live in a hand-
and-mouth way, upon inconceivably little, a mere
pittance, that is an object with none to supply, and
which stimulates nothing. The agriculture of England shows us what a home market can effect.
That country, whose soil by nature is poor and moist,
fit only for grass, and becomes a grain country only
by intense manuring, and such efforts to counteract
its moisture and cold character, is now a garden. It
is the most substantially cultivated country in the
world, taken in connection with the neatness, style,
comfort, and independence of the inhabitants. The
home market is the magic that accomplished all
this. The certainty, steadiness, and high prices of
the home supply, have converted a cold, moist, in-
clement soil into a garden, the pride of their country; shining as it does with its neat cottages, tow-
ering spires, and meeting the eye every where with
its substantial wealth and lordly comfort. I do
not say that it is right to build up a home market
at such a sacrifice as the corn laws have created
for them. Our agriculture, with our soil and climate, would flourish under a hundredth part of the
impulse she gave to hers, and we could grow rich
on one-fourth of the prices paid there—we could

give to ours all possible extent and productiveness, without taxing any other business; without the curses of the impoverished operatives; indeed, it would follow and obey all the movements, and be affected by all the operations of manufactures, and be sufficiently stimulated by their prosperity. Without the aid of a home market our agriculture would be the semi-barbarous, log-cabin state described above, without pride, style, or taste, and an entire stranger to wealth and the higher enjoyments. This would shut in all the prospects of industry; beyond there would be no hopes, no aspirations, but a fixed state of semi-barbarism to the Americans; what the tent is to the Tartar, or the wigwam to the Indian, in which whole generations grow up, without refinement or taste, and what is worse, without any advance in the great march of civilization. For all which they substitute fighting, and drinking, and gambling, and hunting. As soon as you give to agriculture a market, they become proud, generous, refined, and hospitable. Having the means, they become educated, and throw around their houses and gardens decorations and shrubbery, get fine furniture, and live in social refinement. Such agriculturists have the information to make them valuable to their country, the pride to have their rights respected, and really become the substantial yeomanry of which we have heard so much. Manufactures, therefore, are invaluable to agriculture, by furnishing this home market, by stimulating and ensuring to them fair prices for

their products, particularly provisions, and insti-
tuting that beautiful system of mutual dependence
and supply, that takes up all the productions, however varied, and all the goods fabricated. There is
nothing so pleasing, varied, and enriching as this
barter ; nothing so certain in its operation, so comfortable in its consequences, and so sure in its results. The flour trade, one of the heaviest, most
bulky, and valuable, is already vastly stimulated
by our manufactories, as few as they are. We sell
now more than twice as much flour to them as we
export, not less than one million barrels ; corn,
pork, beef, bacon, potatoes, and fish, in the same
proportions. The best estimates taken from our
census, and from such facts as the large and concentrated establishments of that kind furnish, show
us that our agriculturists sell of heavy, bulky products, such as flour, corn, pork, beef, rye, buckwheat, oats, barley, rice, fish, potatoes, and butter,
cheese, fowls, and all the small cultures, not less
than twenty million dollars worth to our manufactories. This estimate is no doubt far under the
mark, if we include the thousands of interchanges
that each settlement carries on that cannot be noticed, such as the thousands of smiths, shoemakers,
tailors, wagon-makers, gunsmiths, and the like, that
are scattered through each and every settlement.

  Cotton. Let us now see how the great staples
would be affected by the establishing of manufactories. The portion of them that constitute raw
materials are of course favorably affected, and im-

mediately allied with, or entering into, the operation
on reciprocal principles. We will begin with cotton.
After the full history and account that we have entered into.in reference to the growth, production,
and price of this great staple, we need say but little. It is the great interest of this country emphatically, and worth all the others. It is the resource
of the whole country, fills our coffers, employs our
ships, takes up our capital, and furnishes one-half
of the whole ability that we have, or that we wield
abroad, and enables us to buy what we ought to
make at home. This staple has perhaps done harm
in this respect; for, if we had it not all the time,
we could not have continued to buy so much from
Europe, and would long ere this have made at home
all we needed. Nothing will be more benefited,
however, by manufactories, than this great staple.
It will then have a home market; and, as we said
before, there will be a competition that will benefit
the growers of it. As a raw material, its very life
and soul is consumption. The interchanges it will
lead to, the numerous agents necessary to buy and
forward this bulky article, the vast amount of tonnage necessary to convey it to the places where it is
wanted, the diffusion of the goods made to the interior, through our railroads and canals, all together
give to it a consequence that no other staple production possesses. It would be hard to calculate
the thousands of interests affected, the thousands of
springs of industry it will touch and stimulate, and
the thousands of persons to whom it will not only

give employment, but enrich. The general effect, too, on the whole nation, its resources and independence, politically speaking, will be great. There is no interest that ought to hail the establishment of manufactures louder than this, both in reference to its supplies and markets; yet nearly all the growers of this great staple are extremely hostile to manufactures. It is discouraging to a patriot and a political economist to see this hostility from so enlightened a source; to see that prejudices and party do carry on blindly a whole people to the most suicidal acts, without giving them time to think and calculate their own interests. The shelves of every merchant would convince them, if they would look, that all their supplies are already cheaper, and better in quality, and better fitted for their purposes, than they were formerly; and this brought about by a partial or very imperfect carrying on of manufactures. Their own factors tell them that the American spinners, by their competition, are worth annually two cents to the cotton market. Reason, too, tells us that a great deal more cotton is used now by the circumstance of the Americans making coarse goods, weighing heavier, and out of our own cotton, than would be if we got those things from England, because she would make them much lighter and out of the worthless Surats. Our taking the coarse goods market from England will banish altogether these Surats, because they will not do for fine goods such as then would be left to England to make.

Every point of view in which an inquiring mind would look at this subject, would lead to the conviction that the cotton culture would be more benefited by a tariff than any other.   It would derive some benefit in having the agriculture taken up in provisions, leaving it less overdone, or somewhat unclogged, by having a part of those engaged drawn off, and leaving room to the slaves residing in those districts to remain there, instead of moving south to clog the cotton culture.   When a people, however, take a set on party feeling, nothing can convince them ; and so prejudiced are their minds, that when benefits do flow in to them, they ascribe them to a wrong cause. They charge the low prices, which are literally the effect of a clogged or overloaded market in regard to cotton, to tariff operations.   Nothing has led me so much to despair of this country and its institutions, as the want of thought and the right understanding of their interests that these otherwise enlightened and independent cotton growers have manifested, and their disposition, in the most reckless way, to throw all to the four winds, and their own interests among them.   Manufactures cannot fail to benefit all raw materials.   An increased consumption of cotton in any part of the globe, in the present free and enterprising intercourse, will be useful, because markets find their level; and let a vacuum or demand be created in any quarter of the globe, the article would rush in to fill it.

Tobacco.   Tobacco, as an article of luxury,

which it is, would be benefited by the establishment of manufactures. In a condensed population
and a social state, snuffing and smoking particularly would be greatly promoted. Tobacco being an
article of luxury, its use can be dispensed with
whenever the circumstances or funds of the individuals are limited. Manufactures would give to
thousands the ability to enjoy this raw material,
and its consumption would be much increased.
As a raw material, however, it enters into sundry
manufactures of its own, such as the stemming of it,
chewing tobacco, snuff, segars, and so forth, employing many hands.   This staple culture takes up
most of the slaves of Virginia, Maryland, Kentucky,
and Missouri, and would be as much relieved as
any other staple by drawing off any labor from it,
or diverting still more from entering it.   It is an
overdone and clogged market now, and should join
in the establishment of manufactures in order to
free it, secure to it a living profit, and some increased consumption.   Europe encourages our tobacco staple, by prohibiting their own people its
culture, with a view to levy a tax on its introduction.   Strange to say, this staple is worth to the
exchequers of England, France, and Germany,
thirty million pounds a year, a sum that would buy,
twice over, the whole body of it here where grown.
Any revolution that would disturb the monopolies
in Europe of this article, and allow it to be cultivated there, (for all these countries favor its growth,)

would prostrate the whole interest here, and almost wipe it away as a staple.

Rice.   Rice, as a staple, will be favorably affected by manufactures.   It is considered by the laboring population in Europe and America as an article of luxury, but in the East as an article of necessity, and the cheapest of all food.   Taking it in its character of a luxury, the consumption will increase with the ability to buy it; and with the elegance that a people wish to give to their diet, and much more of it, therefore, will be used in the manufacturing districts.   The price of it is as low as that of any grain, and at the same time more variety given to it in the routine of cookery. It is also a healthy food, and wherever it appears, rather indicates a style of living above the ordinary vulgar one that runs with laboring people.   There might be a beautiful barter instituted between the Carolinas and Georgia, that grow rice, and New England, that manufactures, and that might be led to consume largely of it.   Many of the flour districts that furnish our manufacturers with that article, such as the Genesee country, in New-York, are so much taken up themselves with manufactures, that they want very little of that sort of things, and have to be paid in specie for their flour. That never could happen between the manufacturers and the rice planters; the latter would want all the time for their rice, domestic goods; and the mutual principle of barter would be permanently established between them, to the benefit of both. If the manufacturers could get into the habit of eating boiled rice in place of bread with all their meals, the consumption of rice would increase much, and a better food in the bread way, as well as a cheaper one, be established. When the habit of taking boiled rice with meat, and butter, and milk is formed, it is never changed, and they become fonder of it, than of either corn or wheat bread. Rice costing two cents a pound is cheaper than corn meal at eighty cents a bushel, or flour at four dollars a barrel; is easier transported and handled, and every way easier prepared in cookery. I think those who are concerned in feeding operatives and laborers, would find their account in every way, in introducing its use. Whatever is cheapest and best, is almost sure to be found out by our enterprising people, and I may take it for granted that the staple of rice is destined to be still more benefited by the introduction of manufactures.

Hemp and Flax. Hemp and Flax are raw materials, and destined to be greatly benefited by the introduction of manufactures. Already the hemp interest is far advanced, for we make nearly all our cotton bagging, amounting, for three million bales, to eighteen million yards, and all the cordage or rope to bind them, out of our own hemp. We are now aiming to supply our navy and marine with hemp and every thing hempen, and all the rope used for a thousand purposes, in agriculture, commerce, and manufactures. Hemp is about to be exported as a raw material, and, at three to four dollars a hundred, can be taken to Europe and sold alongside of the Russian in all their markets. Kentucky and Missouri, supposing its culture confined to slavery and rich land, can furnish any amount wanted. As the prices of tobacco and provisions go down, or become dull and uncertain, will those states go to hemp as a resource, or rather an alternative for slave labor. They will thus vary their production, and find their account in it. I have known districts grow rich by having two or three staple productions to lean upon, and always hitting a good market with one or another of them. Hemp is a very exhausting crop, and unless the soil be of the deepest limestone fertility, naturally, will not endure its culture long. The soil in the two states of Kentucky and Missouri is literally inexhaustible, and can stand the hemp and tobacco culture all the time. Those states too are deeply imbued with slavery, and under a treatment in regard to them, that will insure a vast increase of that sort of labor. The hemp crop, therefore, being furnished both with a soil and suitable labor, and stimulated, in addition, by the wants of manufacturers, who will pay for it in a sort of goods that will be wanted in those states, will insure it a valuable product to them, and a great resource to the country. The flax can be produced in any part of the United States, and by either slave or free labor.

When the article is wanted, either as a valuable export or raw material, it can be furnished in any quantity.

If a protecting tariff should insure the making of linen up to the consumption of this country, and all things made of flax, it would stimulate its culture, and render it quite a staple production; not only to supply a valuable raw material, but for export. Several raw staples have not in this country become much cultivated, until some manufacture started up that required them. Then the country is put upon its resources, and gives such attention to them, as to bring them rapidly into notice. This has been the case with hemp, and will with flax, when we shall have advanced a few steps further. When wanted for consumption at home, the supply is sure to go beyond the wants [of the manufacturers, and become an article for export. An invention is now in successful operation that cards the flax and cotton together, and makes a very pleasant sort of goods, which will be extensively used for summer, because both lighter and cooler than cotton goods. In the present populous nature of Ireland, a state where all its soil will be wanted for provisions, she will not be able to grow raw materials—will procure raw flax in this country, and save the soil necessary to grow it on. The fact that she cannot spare soil enough to ripen her seed upon, is a proof that she would not spare soil to it at all, if she could get her supply elsewhere; for flax that matures its seed, does not make a fine, soft, white goods ; it has to be cut green, or unripe, to have the lint very fine ; and hence their habit of procuring the seed from this country. A fortiori we could make still more profit by preparing the lint than the seed, and will do it when any thing at home stimulates its production.

Silk. Silk is going to be produced in this country in vast amount and of a good quality. The experiments already made go to show that the climate, from New England to Louisiana, is suited to the growth of both the worms and the tree that they feed upon. We are already under way, and we will make this year half a million pounds of raw silk, and manufacture it all into sewing-silk and clothing. Several states have, in their individual capacity, offered bounties for the production of raw silk, and it may now be regarded as a certain great staple culture of this wide region ; and not only furnishing raw material enough for the goods that we consume, but a vast raw staple for export. We have extra labor enough to grow all the silk that England and the north of Europe need, cheaper, and of a better quality than Italy and France can furnish. The sort of labor that we are putting to the silk culture, consists of women and children, such as will not be missed from our agricultural operations. Experience supports this sort of a calculation, in reference to the silk culture ; two acres of land are enough to grow trees upon, necessary to feed with certainty and ease worms enough to produce fifty pounds of raw silk in the hank; and six weeks the time necessary to feed the worms that make it. The wife of a peasant or farmer and the children make the silk —the emolument is theirs; they stop their school for the six weeks only, the feeding time, and none of the operations of the farm are interfered with by the operation, nor of their schooling. The wife and children make from three to five hundred dollars a year, which is a resource for books, fine things, and pin money, and gives a sort of independence very gratifying to them. This thing is proved in the above way, and is sure to work up into a vast raw staple, both for manufacturing purposes at home, and a large export abroad. Say that half a million families make their fifty pounds seach, it amounts to twenty-five million pounds; an amount more than England manufactures, with all her preparation and effort. If we should by a protecting tariff stimulate this thing, it would go immediately up to this point—is sure to go ahead after the experiments already made, and is sure to be a vast resource to this country. If this nation could see the great, and rich, and elegant resource it has in both the cultivation and manufacturing of silk, she would immediately engage in both. Looking forward to what a few years will produce, a very pleasing picture presents itself to our view; that gives the certainty of one of the richest, most valuable, and elegant staples in the world. Here, too, were it necessary, slave labor could be well employed, and fill up any vacuum that might occur in it, or be felt in relation to its labor. Such a field cannot remain uncultivated, and it will be seen whether our Congress will have the foresight and the sound policy to insure the double shape of wealth that is ready to flow from it, the wrought and raw value both. When a nation engages in the cultivation and making of silk goods, it is indicative of a state of refinement in the taste, and an advancement in the civilization of its people, and connects it with all the luxuries and elegancies of life.

Labor. The labor of the country of course, above all other things and resources, will be benefited by a protecting tariff. This is the creative genius that it calls into existence, and with which it works the wonders and magic that astonish and enrich. Something comes so nearly out of nothing under the operations of labor and industry, that we ought to look upon them not only with favor and protection, but with a sort of grateful feeling, as our very life's blood. It not only costs a people nothing to labor and produce, but is a pleasure, and a sure guaranty for not only the wealth created, but order and morality, and we may add health. Labor is the foundation of all wealth and all capital, and the only inherent available resource that appertains to man. What avails a rich soil and a fine climate, and fuel, and animals, if there be no labor to develope them? no skill to fashion or mould them into useful forms? Labor makes the capital and wealth, and capital doubles back upon labor, its creator, and gives to it still more efficiency and productiveness by preparations in machinery and power. The capital issuing or springing from labor, is not the ungrateful offspring; it continually lends its aid, purchases protections, and secures new markets to productions. The ratio existing between labor and capital becomes geometrical in its operations, and by this kind of reciprocal action they go on to an almost unlimited existence. Hence, when a wise or fortunate nation gets the start of all others in the great operations of manufactures, commerce, and even in agriculture, it keeps it; and not only keeps it, but gives to these great branches of national prosperity a force, a skill, and excellence, that puts the world in requisition. In such a case it becomes doubly necessary to secure the home market by ample protection to the countries that are behind, and in a manner subject to the superior start and action of that fortunate one. Nothing but protection will then break the spell, or rather the chains that hold the one thus outstripped, to its subjugator. It is through this home market protection, that it walks forth to independence first, and afterwards to wealth, and ceases to be the paralyzed customer of its more active neighbor. The first duty, therefore, of all good government, is to look to its labor; insure it not only full occupation, but the greatest productiveness. Political economy abhors idleness worse, if possible, than nature does a vacuum. It is worse than a vacuum, because gravity rushes forth to fill the vacuum; but idleness is a grave where lies dead and

buried the creative genius of man, the means given
to him by the God of Nature to improve his condition.   Most legislators, particularly in this country,
have the cart before the horse.   They inquire,
where are our markets? where can we trade? instead of first looking to and stimulating labor, to
produce or make something for those markets.
They often build ships, or encourage the building of
ships, as we did after our independence, before they
have any thing to carry in them; and parade their
ships, begging to carry for all the world.   All the
world, when wars created difficulties, employed our
tonnage for a short time, but soon found it better to
employ their own, and ours became useless.   We
built towns and ships before we had much trade,
and imported slaves that now embarrass and degrade us, instead of stimulating to the best advantage the native labor of our people.   The first
great questions for a politician are as to the quantity of labor; its productiveness; whether it be
employed to the best advantage; or whether it
could not be better engaged in other fields;
whether it needs stimulus to give to it more effect;
whether it has its market or demand secure and
fixed; and whether even bounties would not draw
it forth to higher efforts and greater excellence.
First of all, he should inquire whether there were
any idle or unemployed persons in the wide land;
and what would turn them in too?   Every hand
wakened up from idleness, and very likely vice, is
a clear gain to the country.   That farmer that

makes one other spear of grass to grow, rears one other animal, makes one yard of goods, one pound of iron, salt, or any other thing or production more, is a benefactor to his country ; and the politician that calls it forth, deserves the thanks and support of that country. That politician who unclogs any branch of overdone business, draws labor from it to others more productive, and secures the proper markets to all new products or operations, deserves double gratitude from the whole country. Why, then, are our politicians and statesmen so very much afraid of touching this point of all legitimate issue; this foundation of all wealth and capital, labor? Why leave it to chances, whilst so much care is manifested for free trade? It would appear to one dropped from another world, unacquainted with all our interests and resources, that our whole Congress or national legislature were taken or subsidized by Europe to favor all their productions or operations exclusively ; even to the total disregarding of those of this country. It would seem to such that Great Britain sat enthroned in all our legislative halls and dictated all their enactments regulating industry and a tariff; and if told otherwise, could not be made to believe that some laws and most important regulations were not the results of bribes on the body politic by the superior wealth and foresight of older and wiser nations. Every idle finger will be pointed some day against those short-sighted and unpatriotic legislators, who left it in sloth, and to vice, and mischief, instead of stimulating it to proper action and usefulness. It seems that our representatives go to Congress to quarrel about the scant imposts, and worthless offices and salaries that are afloat, to judge by their eagerness and graspings for them, without any reference to the good of the whole, or to the regulation and direction of the labor of the country. If they could see and realize the millions of unborn capital, and the wealth, and comfort, and elegance, and taste, that the idle labor now in this country could, if really awakened and rightly directed, produce, they would be astonished, and not fail to do it as a bounden and sacred duty. A politician, to be able to do his duty in a way to redound to the advantage of his country, must study the resources of that country, instead of tricks of demagogues. He must obey the impulse of her wants, rather than party trainings. He must be unprejudiced in his mind, and not forestalled in his principles. He should be open to convictions, and a seeker after truth, facts, and results, and should be ready to seize upon all circumstances as they arise, that might favor the labor and resources of the nation to which he belongs.

Capital. Capital will, as a matter of course, be taken up, and in a permanently profitable way, by the introduction of manufactures. It will be vanted directly for the outfit of machinery, and preparations necessary to put in requisition the idle labor of the country. That labor would not only divide nterest for the capitalists, but a profit and support for itself. Capital when not permanently invested, merely seeking interest annually, is almost sure to do more harm than good, because those branches most depressed and in debt, are the first to come forward to take offered loans, to pay their old debts, under a hope their business will revive so as to justify the transaction. Alas! soon they become convinced that the capitalist will absorb all and end in a break up for both. The indebted turns over his stock and substance to the loaner, who sees when too late that the stock turned over or closed upon, will be dead capital, and never reimburse the loan. Now that agriculture is so much overdone in all its varied productions, and all the stocks of the numerous banks too high and unsafe for certain investment, including those of the state loans, the capitalists are very desirous of some safe and permanent object on which to employ their money. This, therefore, is the proper moment for the adoption of a protecting tariff, to give employment to this capital, and induce it into channels that would not only promise a profit to it, but the developement of national resources. A country must feel more content with its capitalists, when it sees them so completely identified with its labor, resources, and raw materials, and feel some guaranty that it is working good. It is the part of a wise and patriotic statesman to so arrange the capital of his country, that it is sure to rise or fall with the country, so as to make it the interest of the owners that the country should be steady, orderly, and undisturbed by changes of any sort. Capitalists then stand upon the watchtowers, the great policies of the nation, and guard its best and most substantial interests, by giving early notice of any deterioration in the markets, any hazards that threaten, or any injurious operation of laws or regulations that need change or alteration.

When the capitalists who control the labor and operations of a country reside abroad, and have of course the bulk of their means where they do reside, and any conflictions arise between the country they properly belong to, and the one where they have incidentally a small portion invested, they become governed by their leading interest, and let the smaller go. When, on the contrary, they are wholly identified with their nation and proper country, they do battle for it, and exert vast influences upon its course. A strong illustration of this is found in the English government, where the body of her capital is invested in her eight hundred millions of national debt. They not only aid in keeping her up with their personal efforts, but advance still more of their capital to insure the safety of the other. Her national debt, in regard to national safety, becomes an arch of strength; the more weight, in reason, put upon it, the firmer it is, and the steadier it bears. A protecting tariff would induce much capital to come from abroad, seeking investment of a permanent character. So great is the abundance of money in England now, interest only two to three per cent., that much of it would

.flow hither, if a tolerable prospect were held out to
it. This would be of no small advantage to this
country, and insure it the means of employing all
its labor, and developing every resource. A double
duty devolves on politicians and statesmen, that of
first protecting, and rendering effectual, labor, the
basis of wealth; and when that wealth or capital
is realized, of protecting it, and offering it employment in every possible way at home. This prevents it seeking investments abroad, and becoming
alienated from the country, and in a manner alien-
ating its owners too, for " where the treasure is
there is the heart also." A person is in the
nature of a hermaphrodite citizen who has his interests divided between his own and other countries.
His patriotism is divided, and his services cannot be
counted on. If any thing happens to that country,
he calls on his government to interfere and protect
his interests there, and frequently is the means of
involving it in war, or alliances of a doubtful or
injurious character.

Iron, Coal, Copper, Lead, &c. The iron and
coal, lead and copper, and other minerals, including
the clays and alkalies, are immediately concerned
in a protecting tariff. They would all be first developed as raw materials, and then enter deeply into
nearly all sorts of manufactures. No class of raw
materials furnish so much and contribute so much
to success in all branches, where labor is engaged,
and all abound in our country. The iron and the
coal lie together, and can blow into existence at

the first blast, all the raw materials necessary to a thousand other branches of manufactures, and in this compound ratio become a double source of profit. Were these very useful materials uncovered and brought into actual bright existence by a tariff, we would go on to such an excess, as would swell the volume of our raw materials for export to a vast amount. The world has so much use for these valuable products, and in many countries they are worked to such disadvantage and at such expense, that a great market would open for them. One iron mountain of fine ore, in Missouri alone, yielding seventy per cent. of the purest malleable iron, could supply the whole world, if rightly worked. Equally abundant is the coal, copper, lead, salt, clay, marble, and all such things. This country, like a young giant, knows not its strength or its resources, because it has never exerted the one or examined the other. Nothing is wanted to bring forth all this, but a permanent policy, a certainty of protection, a security of the home market. All would then come forth and show themselves; capital, labor, raw materials, a market, wealth, comfort, elegance, taste, and independence. As soon as confidence was established, they would flash forth, as the gas lights when touched by a match. No country is underlaid so universally with valuable minerals; and they lie in its extended fletz or secondary formation in horizontal strata, that can be followed into the thousands of hills and ridges; and lying above the valleys, can be poured forth, without shafts or drainings, to the fertile plains, water powers, and navigations that are there found. Had this young giant, with its free limbs, hold of these mines of wealth, in the real skilful way, she could glut or monopolize all markets, both in the raw and wrought state. These hidden treasures need a protecting tariff to uncover them, its inducement to make them available, and wiser statesmen than we yet have, to put all in train, and on the certainty of the reality.

Internal Improvements. Our internal improvements, railroads, and canals, and steamboats, would be benefited by the establishment of manufactures, for the transportation on them would be more voluminous and varied. The raw materials give much more support to lines of intercommunication, than the wrought goods that a country needs. In the carrying of raw materials and agricultural supplies to our manufacturers, and interchanging with them for their goods, the whole operation is American, and as gratifying as profitable to Americans. When, however, a sneaking and selfish foreigner uses them to start along his flimsy dry goods, perhaps half smuggled in, too light and useless to pay much toll, yet valuable enough to greatly tax our industry, if bought and used, the scene becomes changed, and the patriot feels that such great works are prostituted to unworthy purposes, for which they should not be constructed or intended. The interchanges that would go on be-

tween the agriculturists and manufacturers, and
the growers or producers of the raw materials, and
those who give to them available shapes, or ship
them off to a foreign market, would be great, and
offer a most pleasing picture of prosperity. The
capitalists interested in these works of improvement
then would feel that they were subserving the
whole country, were the very arteries that gave
diffusion to the very heart's blood of the country's
industry, and that they were finding a profitable
dividend from their investments in them. Such
works are the proper handmaids of a home market and home industry, and enable them to meet
the demand at all the points, and in every shape.

There is something wrong, when we see a people entering upon great works of intercommunication, before they have developed their resources in
agriculture and manufactures. It is like letting
an enemy into the heart of the country, a serpent
into our very bosoms. Some foreign nations then
do not fail to rush in their productions and goods
upon such invitations, and through such openings,
to the forestalling of the market, and if unchecked,
to the prevention of any domestic supply. When a
nation is ready for meeting its home supplies, and
wishes to bring the raw material and the manufactories together in a cheap and rapid way, or the
agricultural provisions in contact and barter with
the articles of our manufacturers, then all facility
should be given. Again, when wine and provision districts, which of all others most need inter-

change, require to be brought together, or when valuable minerals, iron, coal, lead, copper, zinc, clay, and such things, in train of development, and required by the manufacturers, need to be brought forth for use and interchange, or when agricultural products find it to their interest to look abroad for a market, and require to be brought cheaply to the seaports for shipment, then in all such cases these roads, and canals, and carrying boats, should be constructed, and the country will find its account in it. Build not for your rivals, open not your doors until you know who or what is to enter, are wholesome adages, and comport with common prudence.

The impulses of liberty often carry us too far in reference to other things. We feel free and at liberty to act at home as we please, and we naturally extend the privilege to other nations and other people, in their communications with us. Patriotism, we find at last, is something exclusive and selfish, and like charity begins at home; but frequently, before we find that out, our best flowers of commerce have been plucked by foreigners, let into equal advantages as our own citizens. They are apt in such a case to have more than equal advantages, because they stand organized in a way to flood our country with their productions to the exclusion and suppression of our own, and continue to tax us all the time, by the habit of looking to them at first for supplies, that we uncautiously got into. The remoteness from European supply has built up many manufactories in the West, particularly of iron. Then all works we make, and all facilities we create, redound more to others' good than our own. Early modes of supply, becoming a national habit, stay fixed upon us, and we continue them after it becomes our interest to develope our own resources, and supply ourselves. National habits are as obstinate and more so than individual, because it is harder to convince and move a body politic to change them than it is an individual. Politicians should guard against any foreign manner of supplying articles of necessity, and easy modes of getting to a foreign market for them, because the habit springs up of thus getting them, and connects so many interests with it, that it is hard to break it off. We have so many small ties to sever that the great interest, however apparent the call for the change, finds a difficulty in breaking through them; and we often continue to trade to a disadvantage rather than make the necessary effort to change it. Nations are easily lulled to sleep, and in a state of contentedness, when their incomes are very scant, if they never knew a different condition of things; and it takes more stimulants to get them out of such a state than it would to have started them right at first. When a people show energy enough to make a revolution and assert their liberties and rights, then, whilst the spirit is up and the human mind excited, is the time to establish their political economy, and show them the true policy they ought to pursue in regard to trade and manufactures. Their habits then are unfixed, and reason and good sense would be their guide, which, aided by the effort they were then under in regard to their liberties, would easily connect those great interests with it, so as to insure them complete success. Our lines of improvement therefore cannot fail to subserve our manufacturers, and be aided by them in making their dividends on the capital invested, carrying as they would an infinite variety of things, and leading to such multifarious interchanges.

Commerce. Our commerce will be enriched by the establishment of manufactories, as we have said before. The domestic trade, embracing the home market, will take up its capital and its merchants in a more extensive and varied way, and more actively and profitably, when all is of our own growth and production, than it does now at this time. Our tonnage will be much engaged in a coastwise and inland traffic, that will be immensely active, and all of it our own. Our foreign tonnage too will still have the surplus raw materials to carry abroad, and bring back such luxuries as we cannot produce or grow at home, and the great resource of the fisheries to scour after, which will leave it but little impaired. I will venture to say that our commerce will gain more by the active and varied coasting trade, the inland and canal interchanges, the mutual supplies and carryings of the agricultural and manufactured articles,

and the increase of wealth and productions consequent upon them, than it will lose in the foreign
operations.   Quick returns, active interchanges,
safe operations, steadiness of market, equable currency and insurance, and certain, if small, profits,
are the life and soul of all legitimate commerce.
It is in such eternal rounds of active and safe
traffickings that wealth accumulates the most
surely.   In a commerce based upon domestic interchanges more persons and agents, as well as
more tonnage and capital, are employed, and so
connected with it as to gain a living and habits of
business which fit them for useful citizens.   There
is more honesty in a domestic circle of trade and
supply, for character is always at stake, and to be
cherished as an acceptable quality in it; and there
will be less cheating, less defrauding, less smuggling, and glossing over of inferior goods, than in
any foreign trade.

One capital advantage, and worth a thousand factitious ones, is the exemption from overtrading, and
those ruinous vibrations in prices, that an uncertain
commerce leads to.   One time the market is clogged, at another time bare; the thousands rush in
and carry that market immediately to the most op-
posite extremes alike ruinous to the importing merchant, the capitalist, and the consumer. When
an inducement leads to overtrading, millions of
debts are created abroad, and, as we have said, the
banks run down, the specie is borne off, and a general distress invades the land, and ends in as general

a bankruptcy. We showed before that immorality,
discredit, false value, uncertainty, as well as the
loss of capital and specie, attend it. We have seen
more money lost in one fatal year than we gained
in half a dozen. Our foreign commerce, too, is invaded by wars, blockades, the dangers of the seas,
the changes of duties, and the whims of other nations; whilst our own domestic intercourse lies snug
in port, or glides safely from place to place, alike
secure from the weather, the enemy, and overtrading. Commerce has as deep an interest in securing the home market and supply as manufactures can have—they are both taken up in supplying it, par nobile sororum. Less money is necessary
to conduct the home operations, because our credit
is more available near home, and most of the commerce is a mere barter or exchange; whereas, in a
foreign trade, specie has often to go and lie out of
an interest pending the voyage. The money exchanges too are less affected in a home trade, for
we know the market better, what its condition and
supply is, govern ourselves accordingly, and are
never thrown so much out as to pay much for exchange. When commerce confines itself to a legitimate home trade, mostly of a barter or exchange
character, it needs but little ready money, and
leaves the more for other purposes, with which to
establish manufactories for instance, to uncover
the valuable minerals of the country, or go into
plate, and luxuries of taste and living, which make
the wealth of a country. Commerce has no patri-

otism in it, when based upon foreign supplies. Its reachings are often illegitimate, and its profits comport not with the prosperity of any one country. It is a cosmopolite, and cannot feel devotedly, cannot act exclusively, nor make sacrifices for any country. Of all occupations and professions it is the one that ought most to love and be the readiest to lay a helping hand to its proper country; and ought, therefore, to trade exclusively in that country's productions. Banks become sure depositories, ready aids of business operations, in the short-loan way; and centres for the employment of active capital, when not under the influences and fluctuations of foreign trade, leading to overtrade. Capital derives its powers of accumulation from labor made productive, and is of course deeply concerned in, and benefited by, a protecting tariff, that would enable labor not only to employ it, but insure its increase.

Currency, Specie, and Banks. The currency, circulation, specie, and banking operations of the country, would, as a whole, or in severalty, be greatly benefited by a protecting tariff. Such a tariff would, as we have seen, give employment and accumulation to capital;—I will here add, will give a sound and steady currency, and a circulation as sound, and based upon specie. The banks, the proper guardians and depositories of the money, would issue those deposits in convertible paper, that would give facility in carrying from place to place, or, what is still better, exchanges; and keep the whole up in a steady and equable value that would be felt. No overreachings or overtradings to derange this convertible currency, cast suspicion on it, make runs on the banks, or drafts of specie. All would go on smoothly, and the regulating spring being in this country instead of Europe, would be under our own control. Speculation must have a wide field where the imagination must have room to act, and uncertainty appertain to the operation, before it runs wild, and endangers wholesome trade, changes values and exchanges. In a close, home, snug market, all its demands and supplies are understood, all its wants known to all, and all its capacities calculated every day or month, and met accordingly, without excitement or derangement. Speculation runs wild in reference to foreign markets, scarcely ever the home. Circulation, and currency, and banks, and exchange are the indices of a steady, wholesome market, or an uncertain foreign one, as they are affected. An alarm in commerce, like the panics often encountered in armies, spreads from uncertain action or small causes, when darkness or confusion prevents the true character of the danger being seen, and gathers force by its own derangement, until all are prostrated before its wild bearings. A specie basis is the true one for a circulating currency, so long as trade is without excitement, or its balances undisturbed; but when speculation sweeps along with its alarms and runs, this specie basis, like the rock foundation of a fine building in an earthquake, is soonest upheaved and thrown prostrate. It is not the foundation that we can mend, but the cause of the overthrow avoid. Those nations are to be envied, that go along the plain high road to wealth and comfort, under safe operations of labor and commerce, and keep in the proper channels and in equal values, not only the currency concerned and the exchanges, but the values of all the commodities that are' the objects of the daily exchanges and operations.

Independence. The independence of our country will be deeply benefited, and placed on a firm and secure footing, by a protecting tariff. I have shown that we still have to depend on foreign markets for many articles of the first necessity, and for nearly all of our luxuries. The important and every day indispensable articles of iron, steel, salt, coal, copper, blankets, flannels, carpetings, saltpetre, and such other things, are not (to the shame of the country be it said) yet made at home, up to more than one-half of the consumption. I have shown that in the last war with England, we had not these things, and had to take them from our enemy under a license disgraceful in its character, and still more disgracefully connived at by our government. Near thirty years have since elapsed, and we do not yet make and produce these things. This puts to outrage all experience and sufferings on this subject, and our better knowledge of the facts goes for nothing. What is any government worth in the public estimation, that would let an occasion of this kind pass as a thing of course, and not profit by its lessons? All our luxuries, both of the table and style, stand back; none furnished at home—all got abroad. No citizen can pretend to style and taste, and the comforts and elegances of a gentleman, without filling his house, his cellar, and ornamenting his person, from abroad. Were all these things made and produced at home, we would all have a prouder feeling, a more independent and bold manner, and be better patriots and citizens, and then only feel and act like true Americans. We could then lean upon the bosom of a rich, and honored, and refined country, and try to be worthy of it. Had we not seen and felt the truth of the fact, we never a priori would have believed for a moment, that any nation would, by a brave and bold effort, establish liberty and independence, without immediately, as a first principle, looking to and insuring, by proper laws and protection, the production of all things necessary to the daily wants of the people, and the independence and defences of its government. These United States have too truly shown a case to the contrary of all this; and, after a struggle that called down the applause of all the world upon them, have slouched on in their productions and consumptions, as it were by accident, regardless of any system that covered their wants, secured their independence, and guaranteed wealth. When we did awake to these things, we found our hands manacled by foreign ties and bonds, and domestic **party**

spirit, in such a way that we could not act.   Selfish and interested foreigners were offering sacrifices
upon our altars and desecrating our hearths, that
should have been free and sacred to our own people
only.   We were told to sleep on ; they would take
care of our valuable staples, and vouchsafe a supply of goods to us on their terms.   Like the young
and dissipated spendthrift, we sink back into sloth
and inefficiency, and leave all to chance, or what
is worse, to interested counsellors.   The feelings
of pride, as we said, that run with a full and elegant supply of all we want, are very important to
a nation, and awaken patriotism and love of country.   We look with but little satisfaction on the fine
things around us, unless we can feel that they are
a part of our country, and supplied at home.
Among the civilized nations of the world, we are
the only one that depends for articles of defence, of
war, of independence, and for daily consumption,
on foreign countries—perhaps on enemies.   Why
have we earned this not proud but strange and
dear-bought distinction ?   Can we afford to act
differently from the rest of the world, and put at
nought all experience, all reason upon the subject ?
We have not the inherent energy and union of action that can dispense with such aids.   We are a
divided, scattered, and undecided people on all
emergencies, and need all these facilities to give us
any means of prompt action, where our rights are
invaded.   We have had to bear with insults for
years, and leave them unresented, because we knew

that we had not the things necessary to war and defence, and because we felt that our population would suffer during the struggle, for most of the necessaries, and all the luxuries. Witness the ten years of insult before we fought England the last time, and then, owing to our divisions in relation to manufactures, began the contest in our shirts, totally unprepared.

Information. Information will be improved by the establishment of manufactories, and morality not injuriously affected, nor the health or constitution impaired, when carried on as done in New England. In order to apply the Lancastrian monitorial system of education to any population, it is necessary to have them condensed into close settlements. This very sweeping, cheap, and efficient plan cannot follow people into the woods; cannot flourish on the frontier, where they could not be gathered together, and made to teach each other, and sympathize together. In the manufacturing villages the children, proper subjects for this sort of school, are crowded together, and can be collected at the ringing of a bell, enough to fill the largest sort of a room. A little money serves for the purpose; and the human mind advances to usefulness and information in solid column, supported by each other's sympathies. At night, when the day's labor is over, the ringing of the same bell will call the adults, male and female, not to gin shops, but to lecture rooms, filled with books, apparatus, and specimens, and a lecturer, that can engage,

amuse, and instruct them.   If the selfishness of the
English capitalists, owners of the factories, had not
been in the way, and a start taken of the gin
shops by these schools and lectures, their operatives would not at this day be so degraded, ignorant, and dissipated.   They would have found
amusement as well as the delights of information in
these rooms, and been a more valuable and useful
class.   In this country we carry the facility of information and of education into the factory villages
and towns, and find it effectual.   The rising generation are all taught; the adults attend lectures,
and become even scientific.   Self-esteem and the
moral principle take hold of them, and lead to a
care and providence that instantly banish want
and suffering, and pretty much dissipation and vice.
The philanthropists connected with these New
England manufacturing villages now challenge
a comparison between their operatives and the
same number of agriculturists in that or any
country, both as to information, taste, decency,
providence, and virtue; and very disinterested persons do not hesitate to say that all is in favor of the
operatives.   We have lost nothing, then, in morality, have gained much in decency and taste, much
in providence and care, much in character, and even
religion.   I may add as last, but not least, that they
have still greater and more striking advantages in
wealth and productiveness.

   We have now gone over the whole ground, examined every interest candidly and fairly, and

seen that the introduction of manufactures by a protecting tariff would subserve and promote all, collectively and severally. The reasoning, facts, and arguments brought forward, will be conclusive to the minds of all that are unprejudiced, and take time to examine them. To the patriot, a picture of prosperity and national independence is presented that cannot fail to please and delight him,—to the statesman, enough to bring him into the support of all that is wanted to complete and effectuate its realities,—to the agriculturist, a rich harvest and a varied resource,—to the merchant, a better basis of trade, with certain wealth, and fewer dangers,—to the capitalist, a certain and sure employment for his money, and every prospect of an increase of it,—to the slaveholder, some hope of more profit,— and to the manufacturer, the gratitude of his country, as well as a harvest of wealth and comfort. Nothing is wanting but a single act of Congress, giving, in the first instance, the home market, which would be inducement enough to realize the whole, and cover all the ground. Let us up and act, and make our country worth living in.

CHAPTER XIX.

FOREIGN COMMERCE.

LET us now inquire, what political economy, under the present circumstances of our country and

its foreign commerce, should and ought to do for
that commerce, to place it on the proper ground.
We have seen how the establishment of manufactories would affect it, and have inquired whether
it be overdone or not, taken in its present state.
Now we will try to ascertain, whether our foreign
commerce might not be placed on a better footing
than it now stands on, by some enactments of our
Congress, or treaties entered into with foreign governments, in relation thereto. We, or rather our
politicians, or more properly still, our demagogues,
have always been too busy studying party interests, and too much under the influence of party
spirit, to think enough about the great relations of
commerce and manufactures, to understand them,
or know any thing about their bearings. Hence
our manufacturing interests are a foot-ball, continually bandied about, and up and down, until no
one knows on what to count. Our commerce has
taken a little better care of itself; and had it been
left entirely alone, it would by its great activity,
and inherent spring and elasticity, have placed itself on a good footing, or a better one than it now
rests on. We are a great people in our own estimation, and are continually experimenting in regard
to the most practical of all pursuits, commerce.
Our politicians, principally of the Jefferson-demo-
cratic school, hit on, as they thought, a great principle, that of reciprocity; and held it forth to the
commercial world in all the confidence of an em-
piric. Our Congress were so tickled with the idea,

or discovery, that they passed a general law on the subject, directing the executive to place our commerce and shipping upon it, as soon, or as fast as other nations encouraged it. To show the folly of such a principle, and its absolute injustice and imprudence both, let us follow its first steps into fact and practice. We will take it up first in relation to a reciprocity in port charges and tonnage duties. The large commercial nations, our rivals, such as England, France, Russia, Sweden, Portugal, Holland, Belgium, and others, paid no attention to our great principle, and rejected all offers to treat upon that basis, because they had a large active commerce, and chose to keep it under their own control, and such regulations from time to time, as their interests might require. The small states, however, such as Denmark, Hamburgh, Bremen, Prussia, Brazil, Tuscany, Rome, Greece, and the like contemptible governments, without any shipping worth speaking of, caught at the idea of reciprocity, and recognized in it *a great principle.* They, therefore, as soon as offered, made such treaties with us, and they were paraded by our wiseacres to Congress, duly ratified, and as duly puffed. These powers, having little tonnage and less trade, are greatly gainers by the treaty over us, with much tonnage and much trade. Our rival nations, finding things so, slip their tonnage under the flags of these contemptible powers, and send it here free of tonnage duty, whilst all our numerous ships entering their ports, have to pay these duties, which gives them all that advantage over us.   We know how easy this is done by the custom-house leger-demain of all ages and nations.   We will exempli-fy this by a familiar case.   A rich lord and a poor man live near each other.   The poor man says to him, " My dear sir, you have wines, plate, servants, furniture, and stores of all sorts ; I have some things, too, such as splint-bottom chairs, pewter spoons, buckhorn-handled knives, and a good deal of delf and some hard cider.   Now as we both see our friends occasionally, let us reciprocate ; when I see my neighbors, you must lend me your wines, servants, plate, costly linen, furniture, and viands, and when you see your noble friends, I will recip-rocate, and send you my things."   This would be reciprocity with a vengeance ; yet the same sort as exists between us and Bremen, or Leghorn, and others.   Bremen now is highly commercial, sends here hundreds of ships, and occupies a whole range of wharves on the North River in New-York. Hamburgh sweeps the Elbe, and sends out for Prussia, Hanover, Bohemia, Austria, and pretty much all the Baltic states.   Leghorn trades for Italy and Greece, and Brazil and Buenos Ayres for England, as far as South America is concerned.

These few cases show the operations of the great principle of reciprocity as far as tonnage duties go, and prove its short-sighted and impolitic effect upon us.   The great principle is still sung in our legislative halls, and stands on our statute books in all the sacredness of a treaty ; an everlasting record of our weakness and want of thought, or the proper sort of knowledge. Our tariff, as lame as it is, speaks as to the duty on manufactures, but a party stands forth that would put them too on the great principle of reciprocity. Our commerce therefore needs, and loudly calls for, enactments in these respects that will protect our own tonnage and shipping interest, and stand it on a footing that will cherish—not sacrifice it. Sweep me from our national legislature such simple, empty-headed, visionary politicians, or demagogues, that from ignorance are daily overreached, and from party drilling dare not do right when they are told it. It is equally short-sighted to make treaties guaranteeing the advantage of the most favored nation to any one, for we may have a strong motive of interest to offer advantages to some. Our commerce too has lost a very legitimate branch of trade; I do not mean the carrying, for all nations have a right to carry their own productions, but the trade to the ports of nations which they choose to call their colonies. The mother countries, particularly England, and France, and Holland, forbid our going to their colonies with any thing of their growth, or bringing away any thing for shipment to the mother country of colonial growth. We, however, with all the thoughtless indifference imaginable to our own interests, allow those nations to carry our products to their colonies, and from one of our ports to another, without any let or hinderance. We should countervail all these things, correct these one-sided and partial operations, and be true to ourselves and our own commerce. We will not only lose much interest and advantage by this want of discrimination and sharpness, but incur the contempt of all that witness it. Most of our injurious laws and treaties are made, not from a love of free trade, as some pretend, but from absolute ignorance of the subjects, and a want of practical men in our councils. If we were true to our great commercial interests, we would secure the carrying of our huge and voluminous bulk of agricultural and staple productions to all the countries that require them for use. They are valuable and important enough to enter into all treaties and commercial arrangements. Rather than lose them, or have them withheld, all nations would bear any commercial arrangement in regard to them, even if it led to some more charges or cost. England would let us into her colonial trade rather than forego the advantages of carrying our cotton from our country. We are too yielding, short-sighted, simple, ignorant, or not sufficiently practical to reap these harvests when in our way, and avail ourselves of the vantage ground the God of nature has stood us on. When a nation has raw materials valuable enough, staples bulky enough, agricultural productions important enough, and ships enough to affect all the business of the commercial world, and produce spasms or activity as furnished or withheld, thrift or prostration as favored or not, she should avail herself of such vantage ground, such a leverage, to not only build up her

shipping interest and commerce, but obtain through
their operations all the benefits and concessions she
may demand or need. When the fulcrum is furnished by Nature's God to this young Archimedes, it
still fails to move the commercial world. Our commerce, if we demanded it, might double with England around the great capes of South America
and Africa, and sweep the bays of Bengal and
Bombay, scour with her the West Indies, run with
her through all her various colonies, and in every
port, place, colony, or mother country, be a part of
herself as to facilities secured by treaty. No nation could gainsay us, for we would be in possession
of all seas. No nation could war upon us, for we
would be full of resources and wealth. No nation
could countervail us, for we would control all the
productions necessary to her existence. We would
stand on high and enviable ground, placed there by
our own wisdom, that made use of natural advantages and resources too valuable to nations to be
placed on any doubtful footing. This young Hercu-
les, that strangled not the serpent in its early
grasp, will fall like Laocoon in the foldings of its
wrath. Our country has never used to the best
advantage our commercial situation; has not improved the talent given to us; but the rather buried
it under party ignorance and prejudice. Let us
now take hold in earnest of our commercial relations, countervail where necessary, destroy all
mock reciprocity, and show the world that we
must be benefited exactly in proportion to our na-

tural advantages, and the value of our productions
and raw staples.   It will cost us much negotiation,
much bickering, and time, now to correct what
worthless politicians have either done wrongly or
left undone.   It will cost us no war, however ; for
we as customers, and our productions as raw materials and provisions, are too valuable and dear to
other nations to have them jeopardized by a war or
non-intercourse.

CHAPTER XX.

RAW AND WROUGHT VALUES.

The difference between raw and wrought
values is strongly marked and felt in all the operations of producing, fabricating, and trading.   The
raw thing or material is necessarily rough, coarse,
and bulky, implies little value comparatively, and
is generally prepared or produced by a new country and a less refined people, and appertains to a
rude state of the arts and a less skilful population.
It makes up in its bulk to the carrier and the
merchant what it lacks in value, and employs
more tonnage and more agencies in the transportation and disposition of it.   New countries begin
their productions with the raw material and crude
provisions, which pass on for fabrications and consumptions to more skilful countries.   The produc-

tions of a country indicate not only the state of the arts but of refinement,; and the makers of articles of fancy, elegance, and luxury, are necessarily cultivated in their taste. The hands, the axe, hoe, plough, and sickle, produce provisions and staples; a wood-fire blasts the metals; but it requires the finest manipulations, the most delicate and complicated machinery, and some knowledge of mathematics, chemistry, and taste in designing, to create all the fine, elegant, and luxurious articles, such as appertain to the more advanced and refined state of society. The value of the raw material, and the same material when wrought, is as one to five on the average. We are content to be that crude people that roughly produce provisions and raw materials, that enjoy the raw value, and let our more refined neighbors reap the five-fold wrought price; and we weigh ourselves down with roughness, and bulk, and uncouth shapes, whilst our more refined customers display the light, the elegant, and richly beautiful forms of the manufactured goods. Our politicians aspire not to taste, refinement, and the wealth that this five-fold value imparts, but leave us the clodhoppers of the farms, or the hewers of wood in the forests, or the trappers of fur in the mountains, or fishermen, to work along in a naturally rough way, without protection or further inducement. One third part of the people who produce a raw material, cotton, wool, iron, hemp, silk, tobacco, flax, or any other such things, can and do work them up, and impart to them by the operation five values. In plain mathematics, one manufacturer produces in value, or money, five times as much as the one engaged in raising the raw material.   One Englishman, spinning up a given quantity of cotton, earns more than five slaves can in growing it in Louisiana. This is the high ratio that all manufacturing people have rode upon to the wealth and elegance that such nations display, and accounts for that wealth with which England astonishes and subsidizes the world; for in vain may you look for it in her soil and agriculture, and her commerce was merely the medium through which this wealth flowed in and was realized. The commerce of a people, in these times of exclusive right, when each nation sets up to carry its own productions, must depend on what that people produce, and only disposes of it and what it commands from other countries.   Commerce cannot, therefore, enrich a people in the abstract, and can contribute to it only as the medium, agent, or go-between of a population and their productions, and the nations that want them and their trade.   In vain, then, may our politicians allege that England was enriched by her commerce instead of her manufactures, for the latter constituted the very basis and essence of that commerce, called it into existence, and through it realized, not only the value of her manufactures, but a profit on them beyond, in the nature of a tax upon those who consumed them. All the profits of commerce are incidental, and have reference to its basis and support.   Like the light of a satellite, the profits of commerce are borrowed and reflected, not inherent as the centre sun of business, not creative as the producers are.

All the nations of Europe count wealth either as accumulated capital, or as realized in the shape of improvements and luxuries, exactly in proportion as they have manufactories, and through them subsidized the world. They have accumulated wealth faster, when, like England, they connect an active commerce with them, to give to them rapid distribution, and increase the profits on them by a tax on their transportation. The ratio then becomes geometrical, for the basis, which is the goods manufactured, is very profitable, and the charges of the transportation and bartering of them through trade, an additional profit—both operations blending in happily together, and swelling the wealth of the country. It is almost discouraging to see a population laboring at the production of the bulky, and rough, raw product—and some of them too unpleasant for free people to enter on or touch, and leading for that reason to the employment of slaves, the curse of any country—whilst a less amount of laborers are using or working up these raw materials with a comparative ease to themselves, and deriving from them five times the profit that those do who produced them with so much pain. The rough, besweated southerner, the savage backwoodsman, the reckless fisherman, the clodhopping farmer, stand low in any scale of civilization and taste in comparison with the artists. It is no argument against the high profits of manufacturing that its operatives are often poor and distressed, for that is owing to the excess of competition in the capitalists that put them in motion, creating an overloaded market. The wealth derived is as great in the aggregate, and as sure to the coffers of the nation, but so divided that individuals derive nothing but a support after the capitalist receives his dividend. England has occasionally accumulated wealth as fast when the wages of the operatives were low as when they were high; the wealth and profit in the aggregate were the same, but the distribution of it among the producers more unequal. England has, for instance, four hundred millions of money spinning cotton, and makes fifty millions of profit. If she makes that profit with one hundred thousand operatives, or with two hundred thousand, it is the same thing to the nation; not, however, to the operatives individually, for their wages in the one case is double what it is in the other. If, however, she has too much labor, it would be better perhaps to employ two persons at half wages, than one at whole, if the half wages can support them. Half wages are better in all cases than idleness, because that leads to vice, disorder, and suffering. National accumulations stand occasionally on a different footing from the mass of individuals, where the capitalists, as we have said, being few, enjoy the profits, and the laborers being many divide the wages to death, and get a bare support; still these profits and these capitalists are in and of the nation. The only thing that redeems the condition of the producers of the raw material and provisions from the roughness and low profits incident thereto, is the rough sort of independence that runs with it, in regard to the individuals themselves, but not in regard to the nation, its resources and defences. We may look through Europe and verify the fact, that all the rich nations are manufacturers. Often the richest nations are naturally the poorest as to soil and agricultural productions. When any of them are commercial—and most are that manufacture—it is because these very manufactures form the basis of their commerce, the latter being only incidental.

CHAPTER XXI.

NATIONS OF THE WORLD—THEIR CONDITION, AND THE CAUSES.

England. Let us in connection with this subject run over the actual state or condition of each nation of Europe, and see at a glance the character and source of their wealth if rich, or the cause of their poverty if poor. England stands at the head of the list, both for wealth and manufactures. She lives in wealth and luxury, and has capital enough to buy the world, if offered for sale. In other words, she has as much money as all Europe besides. The question naturally arises, How did she acquire it? Not by her agriculture, for the utmost that ever did was to feed and support her, and now does not do that much. Not by her fisheries, for they barely supply her with the luxuries and products of the ocean. Not by working gold, silver, and diamond mines, for she has none of them. It is the fruit of her labor, her manufacturing labor and skill, and the commerce that is based upon it. These have been called into existence by wise policies and protections, and cherished up to the present point, when they are putting the whole world in requisition. These manufactories were aided by iron, coal, copper, and tin mines, which the same wise policy early uncovered, and turned in as invaluable supports to these manufactories. When these things became started and developed, showing some surplus, the same wise policy saw in the insular situation of England great commercial facilities, and sprung an active commerce into existence, under navigation acts and other inducements, in order to trade on and dispose of this surplus. She secured to it a monopoly of all these products of the manufactories and mines, and threw it into an eternal alliance and subservience to them. This commerce carried forth to the new and the old world these artificial productions; supplied all, created new markets when necessary; traded, bartered, gathered in the raw material these factories needed, or money, as the case might be; and returned fraught with wealth and the means of producing more wealth. Her situation, activity, free institutions, and intelligence, soon placed all the new continents in her power as markets; enabled her when it became advisable to conquer the Indies East and West, and create all of them, with their hundred million inhabitants, into consumers and producers of wealth to her. The thing became geometrical as it rolled on; every new fulcrum supported a new and mighty leverage of power that moved a new world, and turned it over to her use and behoof. The capital already accumulated loaned itself to new conquests in order to gain new markets, or created new and mightier navies to secure all her wide conquests and dominions. All of this mighty fabric of English greatness and wealth owes its existence to her manufactories, including her mines, and to the shipping, commerce, trade, and navy that grew out of them, and depended on them for their support and extension, as well as their origin.

We might stop at England, for she furnishes an example strong enough to melt a mountain in the way of conviction, of the unlimited profits and wealth growing out of manufacturing ; especially where a commerce has sprung up based upon it and subservient to it, and a government true to its protection and extension. Pause for a moment and compare England and our country—how wide the difference in their profits and progress ! With not more, on the average, than double our population, she has, since the revolution that brought us into existence, made and realized not less on every estimate than twenty times as much capital to the head as we have. England, her writers say, has a clear income in money, after supplying herself every year, of two hundred millions to add to her capital; whereas we have not one cent, and often fall in debt and behind, after supplying and buying what we ought to make at home. We are now in debt not less than three hundred million of dollars to England for her capital borrowed and lost, and her goods bought for consumption at the time so many of our people were idle and might have made them. England, on the contrary, has the above income and owes not one cent; for her national debt is owed to herself, and in this sense no debt at all. All the world, except France and Holland, owes England; she, nothing. The difference between a nation that has an income, and one with not only no income, but a deficiency and debt instead, is as wide as heaven and earth; indeed, you cannot compare them, for there are no data, no ground to stand on; as well might we compare nothing to something, or subtract nought from millions—there is no result. The above reasoning applies to the capital or income of a people, nationally speaking; not to individuals, for they must live and support themselves in either case, and it is the accumulation of capital, not bread, that is concerned. A nation that outlays one dollar for a raw material and makes it worth five by bestowing labor on it, must realize four dollars by the operation ; no matter how you divide that four dollars between her labor, capital, merchant, or shipping, it is still made and realized. If instead of paying the one dollar for the raw material, she made or produced that too, the whole five then is a creation, a profit, a realization. Here stands this country of ours with labor enough, and much of it idle, to not only produce the raw material that she now does, but to give it the wrought value that counts England so much, and merchants and shipping enough, too, to distribute it all where it might be wanted. If we were to manufacture two hundred million dollars worth of goods annually from our own raw material, in addition to that unbounded raw product, and sell them abroad, superadding to them the profits of transportation and commerce, we would be the richest people on earth. Nothing could then contain our wealth, number our luxuries, or equal our advances in power and influence. Could all this be realized ? It is possible, but very improbable, and hardly desirable. It would enrich us fast enough for our comfort and safety, to move up to our home consumption only, and secure that which is justly ours by the proper laws.

We have slaves enough to produce all the raw staples they now do, and manufacture them also. If then it degrades free people, as some pretend, to manufacture— demoralizes and attenuates them, or renders them sickly—since slavery is really fastened upon us by force of adamantine circumstances, and must be endured, could it not be made to produce all this? Why not try it? Why not make the mighty effort? It would cost no more sacrifice of liberty, or humanity, than it now does. It would then be in its proper sphere, and the forced and imprisoned labor that it must be. All comparisons, then, between England and this country, either fail or end to our disadvantage, both as to policy and productiveness. We are truly and literally now slaves to England, her hewers of wood and drawers of water, and contribute to her exaltation and emolument in every way. We toil and sweat, trudge through mud and mire, sunshine and rain, a burning, deadly climate, and a frozen zone, all to produce invaluable raw materials for England to work up and reap a harvest from. Lest all this might not be enough, we scandalize and disgrace ourselves and posterity, with the foul blot of slavery reaching to millions, in order to insure it. See the American capitalist and master, rough and exposed, worried and fretting, weighed down by the vast bulk of his own productions, and then realizing but a small minimum profit as an individual, and nothing at all nationally speaking, whilst England rolls in wealth! Let us have our work-shops abroad, said the worst politician that ever a nation was cursed with. We have them abroad, by his influence mainly, and our masters are there too; for we have been all the time dependent on them for our necessaries. As well might we say, let our capital be abroad, let our liberty, our independence, be in foreign keeping. Had he lived to the age of a patriarch, under full penitence, he could not have atoned for all the mischief he entailed on this nation, and the disappointment the friends of liberty the world over felt, and are destined to feel, from his visionary acts and policies.

France. France is a rich, cultivated, comfortable, and luxurious country, and rendered so by her manufactures. She had not the commercial advantages of England, nor her free institutions, when she most needed them to start even with her rival. France found a vast resource in her home market, which she leaned on for the first ages of her manufactures. She had also much better agricultural products and in more abundance than England. France had her wine, and oil, and silks, as well as her corn, and meats, and forests, and fisheries, to make valuable interchanges at home. Her provinces were to one another pretty much as foreign countries are to each other, and carried on a vast trade within her own bosom. She had a valuable raw material in silk, as well as wool, plaster of Paris, iron, and many others. If her first efforts, like England, had built harbors, established commerce, uncovered iron and coal, and taken hold of the foreign markets and controlled their supplies, she would have been as rich as England, and shared the world with her. She lacked then the free institutions, the principles of justice, the intelligence, and corresponding enterprise, necessary to such a rivalry. She was so many ages building up free and unshackled institutions, and gaining the spirit, and intelligence, and ambition of commerce and capital, that England had the start of her too far to be overtaken or even imitated. The supplying of the home market and interchanges in France has made her comfortable, luxurious, and independent; and the surplus goods and productions that she exports, though small compared to England, are making her rich; for she has an income, over and above supplying herself, of fifty million dollars annually. In this latter respect she is better off than we are, who have no income, as we showed, after meeting our own wants. England, by estimate, has, and can command in money capital, one hundred times as much as France, in any year, or at any time. Capital is so meagre and scarce in France, that no great objects can be accomplished without aid from England; no stock companies, no extensive loans; all is on a small scale, cautious, and fearful. She either wants capital vastly, or spirit, ambition, and enlightened policy, to wield it. England never slumbered when her interests could be benefited or extended; in peace, she was wide awake; in war, she never forgot her best profits, nor her best markets. Bonaparte was absorbed in his own ambition, and carried France and all her resources into that channel with him. He stimulated nothing but empty glory; he developed nothing but munitions of war; he built no roads, and made no intercommunications, but such as led to conquest and battle; he left no monuments but the Place Vendome, or the Elephant Fountain, both more in memento of his folly than his patriotism; for his great road over the Simplon is the property of Sardinia. He left the corn and wine districts unconnected, which of all others need interchanges the most: he left the coal and iron undeveloped, the only sure basis for manufactures, national wealth, and independence; and manufactures, in the turmoil of war, either suffered stagnation or abandonment. France, however, is a happy country, and wants nothing from foreign lands but a few raw materials and tropical luxuries. Her own bosom is so broad and deep that thousands of interests lie nestled there, and give to her great variety in her own productions and interior commerce.

Holland. Holland now reposes upon her withered laurels as to capital and manufactures; is rich from the past, and snug in her economies, finished comforts, and works. She manufactures not only up to her own supply, but has a large surplus for her millions of subjects in her Asiatic islands and the Indies. Although her income is small and her surplus capital annually not large, with her finished economy she is all the time growing rich. Like England she pushed out her commerce under free institutions and an intelligent spirit, not only to trade in and support her manufactures, but to grasp the riches of the Indies. She at one time was not only the rival of England, but threatened to extinguish her, and it became a struggle of life and death between them; the markets of the world were the prize for which they fought—a very existence the object. England prevailed; Holland sunk back into a second rate power, and became content in following England and picking up the scattered crumbs of wealth and commerce that she left. Her situation has brought her much wealth from Germany. The Rhine, the sea, her economy, her Indian productions, her capital, but above all, her manufactories, made and keep her rich. She caught the mantle of manufactures as the Flemish and Belgians dropped it, and improved upon them. Flanders, failing to have any government until lately, prostrated her pretensions, and her skill and artists took refuge in Holland and flourished. Holland has given to the world a pleasing and useful lesson, not only in economy, but that persevering industry that knew no relaxation, that admitted of no idleness or unproductive capital; the very sea yields to her labors, the very winds are made to work.

Sweden, etc. Sweden has a vast resource in her iron. It procures for her an income, and enables her to purchase what raw materials she needs, and her home market is supplied by her own industry. She has not income enough to enrich herself, but sufficient for her comfort and even luxury. Denmark, Prussia, Austria, Hanover, Bavaria, have no income beyond what supplies their wants. They have, however, secured to their people the home market, and are snug and comfortable, but rather poor nations. They stand on the same footing of this country, without any surplus income. They sell enough, however, of provisions and some raw materials to purchase all they want, and without advancing in the accumulation of capital, or retrograding in the arts, are happy and contented.   The Zollvarien, or Customs' Union, will stand Germany on a better footing, and enrich her.

Russia.   Russia scarcely sells enough of her own productions to supply herself with the many necessaries and luxuries that she needs and does not make.   Hence many parts of her vast empire are laboring under privations, and many of her subjects semi-barbarous, because they have not wherewith to gratify a taste for improvements and the elegances of life.   The emperor has been too much taken up with his own ambition, and the unwieldy and disjointed parts of his heterogeneous dominion, to be able to develope the arts and establish manufactures, even up to the home supply. His powers of combination cannot embrace such an unbounded space.   No one plan or policy can be applied to such widely different climates, interests, and tongues.   Before any general system, no matter how well matured, can cover so many latitudes, it evaporates and is lost.   The Russ knows not the feelings and wants of the Cossack, nor the Tartar of the Calmuck, nor the Fin of the Pole, nor the Courlander of the Siberian ; all must be a random shot, a work of chance, that developes any resource, or that hits any interest, in such a varied, such a wide-spread region.   Such a giant must be stimulated a limb at a time, and dressed up with

the proper appliances in the same way. Were intercommunications established between her disjointed parts, and the proper developments made,
an extensive home trade and barter would spring
up between the parts that produce so differently,
and have such different habits and wants. The
vassals and serfs might, under her absolute power,
be brought in and made into manufacturers, that
would not only supply themselves, but have much
surplus. The hemp, corn, and iron, enable her to
buy much from abroad, and would enrich her, if
she made her own supplies and enjoyed this as an
income.

Small Powers. The small powers of Europe,
such as Hamburgh, Bremen, Frankfort, Ratisbon,
Saxony, Switzerland, are rich from long established manufactures and commerce. They have confined territories, are without agricultural products,
and have found it to their interest to lean on and
give all possible protection to those branches. The
Hanseatic portion have from times immemorial been
commercial. That neutral character and exemption from war, aided by their free institutions that
were early conceded to them, redounded to their
emolument, and insured them wealth and consideration. In the turbulent times of Europe, glimpses
of Asiatic luxuries were caught by the European
savages, as they then were; and the wish to have
them became so strong that a sacred route, threading these towns, was allowed to them to enter
through, without the risk of the wars and rapine

that then seized upon all the avenues of trade and commerce. Under these immunities, those towns accumulated and saved capital enough to give them influence and some control in the affairs of the Germanic body. That capital has swelled by savings, until, in the hands of the Rothschilds and other capitalists, it subserves many great purposes in Europe. The citizens of these free towns were all the time realizing the wrought values, whilst the boorish Germans around them were hardly enjoying the raw. The surpluses of these towns, doubled by trade and commerce, though small, would not fail in five or six centuries to enrich such mere handfuls of population. Switzerland, by having no idle persons, without any agricultural products beyond their own brown bread, has grown comfortable and almost luxurious. Without communications by navigation or easy routes with Europe, she gave a lightness and elegance to her labor in the shape of fine and tasteful articles, that enabled them to bear even mountain transportation, and find and reach a consuming market. Her small annual supplies, with her deep and available economy, has almost enriched her. She is independent, and supplies all her own wants in addition.

Italian States. The Italian States cover their own ground and wants, and have among themselves markets and interchanges enough to insure the comfort and the luxury, if not the wealth, of all. They have a fine climate, and many valuable productions, which find a market, and give the means of some accumulation, particularly in the northern parts of the peninsula. The fine arts have done much for them, and given them income and currency, as well as fame and refinement. The southern parts of Italy, Rome and Naples, and we may include the Grecian States, are so steeped in superstition and indolence, that they have no income, and no ability to purchase from abroad. They have, therefore, to live in a hand-and-mouth meagre way within their own little means, consuming but little in goods, and less in provisions and raw materials. Taste and refinement have been so long shedding their influences upon those districts, that in their very poverty and rags they manifest a people above their situation, abused in politics, and they in turn abusing and misusing their fine country and its natural advantages.

Spain. Spain presents a fine country, full of resources and every sort of advantages, worn down to a mere skeleton by the operation of the worst, most versatile, and despotic government that has ever afflicted Europe. No fixed policy, except the impoverishing one of buying abroad to supply want, has ever marked her course. She is now without income, or any commerce or manufactures that can create one; and hobbles on, half supplied by her own miserable and unprotected industry. She lives, in the midst of great natural resources, in poverty; and, when all the world is advancing in wealth and comfort, she is either stationary, or, even worse, falling back into almost a savage state.

Her lead, her silk, oil, fruit, wine, and mineral productions, as well as all her agriculture, are so much
neglected that they give her but little means to
supply the thousand wants that she does not meet
at home, and she is left in a state of worse than
privation.   She furnishes a striking example of
how poor a country attempting to buy all abroad
becomes, and how helpless from habit and neglect.
Her rich colonies, that poured into her bosom the
precious metals, have set up for themselves, and
these treasures have passed into other and more
efficient hands.   Portugal retains some fragments
of her old trade, and under the patronage and dictation of England, contributes much to the wealth
of her protector.   She has almost no manufactures;   her commerce carried on in foreign bot-
toms, and her valuable wines, fruit, salt and minerals, under the control of England.   She is poor
and without income, and has to limit her wants to
the scantiness of her means, and the unavailing or
unproductive nature of her labor.

Spanish Americas. The Spanish Americas lean
on the mines that lie in their bosom, and buy their
necessaries and luxuries with their products, as far
as they go, without any effort at manufactures or
aim to supply their wants at home.   They buy up
to their means, and do without the rest.   They
have inherited and retained all the indolence of the
mother country, and enough of her pride to render
them totally inefficient.   They will bury, or rather
keep buried, the talent nature gave them, and ex-

hibit to the world a people trying to be free, without the capacity to insure it, and owning a country abounding in all the productions dear to man, as well as underlaid with all the valuable resources, without industry, skill, or intelligence, necessary to develope them.

Brazil and Cuba. Brazil and Cuba lean upon slavery, and have most valuable staples through their operations. They have rich and available productions, mostly tropical luxuries, that all Europe needs and consumes, and fails not to go after and secure. These regions eschew commerce, and lose all the profits that are incident to trade. They merely sell at their own ports these valuable staples, at such price as foreigners choose or can afford to give or pay for them. The great incomes they enjoy are not available as money accumulated, but all go into more slaves, with a view to an increased product. Such an investment may be regarded as an evil, and one that will sink them still deeper into disgrace and embarrassment, when time shall have pronounced upon it. When the bubble bursts, they will find themselves like Hayti, without any wealth or improvements, and in place of them a worthless, degraded, savage population; a population that ceases to produce, not only the staples, but the comforts of life, as soon as the whip of the master is lifted from them. Hayti and the British islands, and Caraccas or Laguira, show, and will prove, that slaves, when let free, are totally unavailable; have not industry enough to make themselves decent, much less to cultivate the staples; and return to the savage state too rapidly for any policy to arrest them, and direct them into the proper channels. Too ignorant to have any inherent impulses that will either form a good government, or originate and obey any wise policy. When the weight of ownership is lifted from such an arch, it crumbles to pieces, and the whole interest falls to the ground. When the stimulus of the whip is withdrawn, there remains nothing to supply its place.

Asia. It is scarcely worth while to travel into Asia or Egypt. Their habits are peculiar, and their wants but few. They run upon extremes in their consumption. The few lords and governors are luxurious; the millions of subjects and slaves want the least possible, both in provisions and clothing. Despotism and rapacity preclude all regular culture or operations based upon a regular investment or commerce. What little capital they possess they hide and bury, to preserve from rapacity; and what enjoyments they have are by stealth. Egypt knows but one big slave-owner, one master, who cultivates cotton as a staple, and sells it on his own account, for a lordly income. There is no hope for people steeped both in ignorance, slavery, and superstition, especially when you superadd indolence and a total destitution of pride and ambition. There are no guarantees there for either persons or property, and nothing worthy of any people can hope to succeed or be attempted.

Hindostan. When we push over further into Asia and reach Hindostan and the Scinde, all is quiet under the leaden and steady purposes of England, and bend to her will. The country has a vast population and great resources, but without factitious wants, or with but little ability to consume ; none where things have to be purchased. England deserves great credit for staying the hand of rapacity, petty discords, and exterminating wars, that swept through that land like a tornado, and threatened all property and all persons. She found the people poor, without much capital, and with few wants ; and though she has hushed the strife, it is a dead and listless calm. So low have those people sunk in the scale of degradation, that nothing can raise them ; so steeped are they in indolence and superstition, that nothing can stimulate them ; so few are their wants, that nothing can induce consumption ; so ignorant, that no light can illuminate such darkness. They oppose no opposition to English measures, yet aid nothing in effectuating them. All that political economy that would premise industry and improvements, and base itself upon the natural or artificial resources of the country must fail, for there is no wisdom to see it, no ambition to excite, nor energy to effectuate any thing available, or produce any result that would go to ameliorate that people or that country. They however make up in the millions of persons for the smallness of their wants, for their total inefficiency, and in that way does England find some resource in them as subjects. England has not acted with her usual foresight in her government of, and policy towards, that people. Had she, by force if necessary, destroyed the fixedness of her casts, wrapped her in European costumes, created new wants in her consumptions, stimulated her pride and ambition, and placed this huge multitude on the high road to civilization and improvement, all that is productive, and industrious, and enriching, would have followed as a matter of course. England would then have insured to herself a leverage that would have moved both the old world and the new. All the tropical luxuries, all the great raw staples would have teemed forth and filled the demands of England up to any increased point, and correspondingly have consumed of English manufactures, until her markets would have been quadrupled. The military chieftains that have issued forth from England and governed Hindostan for the last fifty years, have regarded the diamonds and rupees, and their own personal emolument, rather than the paramount good of England. They thought, when they gained territory, it was enough, without looking to the productions, resources, and consumptions of that territory. They thought that when they counted millions of subjects it was all-sufficient. They received the vast frame exhausted and degraded, and applied no remedies to resuscitate and exalt it. They were willing to stand by and see the cross trampled on; Juggernaut ride over the land, and

funeral pyres inwrap in their flames the innocent
victims, provided they got honors, wealth, and
votes of thanks in the British Parliament.   The
Hindoos, accustomed to rapine and plunder, await-
ed and expected it from their English conquerors;
and instead of hailing the forbearance from these
scenes as the foundation of a new and better state
of things, and as guarantees of security, rather had
a contempt for any conqueror that had not the policy to deprecate, the will to force and appropriate
every thing.   It lulled them, instead of stimulating
them to wealth and productiveness.   Old treaties
or arrangements go to prove that the rajahs and
little kings purchased with sacks of rupees, diamonds, and rubies, the right to retain their religion
in its horrid features, and to continue their rapacity upon their subjects in many cases.   England
cuts not off the thousand heads of this Hydra of superstition, but lets them hiss and poison still the
very fountains of human industry and availability.
Instead of awakening confidence, by direct and immediate protection, she left the population still subject, in many districts, to their own lawless and rapacious rajahs and kings.   England did in this way,
and through such measures, what she dared not do
herself in any direct way.   She saw the people so
poor that no system of taxation based upon European justice and humanity could force out of them
large sums of money, and intervened the native
governors to do the dirty and despotic work.   Now
when the clouds are dispelled, and English author-

ity established beyond all hazard, why does she not new-model those people, and insure some change in their habits, customs, casts, and society, with a view to their amelioration and advancement? When one-tenth part of the population of the globe is thrown by the God of nature and the chances of war under the control and guardianship of any power, a sacred duty devolves on that power to do something for their improvement and happiness.

China. China presents a case every way anomalous and peculiar. She has grown comfortable and even wealthy, in the long run of her existence, on the home trade principally; aided, however, within the last hundred years, by an export of tea and manufactures; or rather a sale of them to Europeans in her own ports. She has bought nothing from abroad until lately, when the eternal embargo has been lifted in part, by British enterprise and intrepidity. She stands ready now to trade with the world on terms that will benefit others more than herself. She knew not what European and American skill could accomplish, aided as it is by machinery, and could not imagine the cheapness with which they can supply her, at the expense of her own industry. A people so teeming with cheap labor as China, ought to buy nothing from abroad. Had she continued the sale of tea and toys in her own ports, for cash only, she would have had all the time a good income, which to a nation buying nothing soon counts wealth and accumulates capital. European and American skill will run her down, and produce still more of distress than her overloaded population already exhibits. She has been thousands of years in accumulating her present scant capital; and unless she restricts her trade and resolves to buy nothing, she will soon lose it all; because when a people are at liberty to buy foreign articles, and find them cheaper and better than their own, they will soon lay out the ready cash they may have on hand.

The trade and commerce of the world are destined to be confined, in the nature of things, to the interchange of such raw materials and productions as cannot be raised or produced by any people at home. The time is coming, if not already at hand, when no article of manufacture will be purchased from abroad, in any civilized country. There will be labor and skill enough in all to produce each and every article, whether of necessity or luxury, and it will be their interest and duty both to do it. The improvements in machinery of the labor-saving sort will be so perfect, that a very small portion of the population, and that of the weakly sort, will be able to manufacture every thing that people want. This will be done without abstracting too much labor from agriculture and the production of raw materials, or at all diminish or jeopardize those great interests. More skill, and labor-saving machinery too, aided by chemistry, will be applied to the productions of the soil, and increase those in a degree little thought of yet. The great agents of steam, the gases, the atmosphere, galvanism, and concentrated chemical manures, will enable the parent earth to produce ten times as much food and support ten times as many people. Labor and skill and power are going to increase faster than the wants or consumptions of the earth. This will insure the idea advanced above, that each and every people will make all they want, especially of fabricated goods. This ultimate state that is fast approaching, will put to flight all the doctrines and operations based on that sort of political economy that goes to make one nation subservient to another, or teaches how to make labor more productive and cheaper in relation to foreign markets and foreign supplies. But one tariff law or regulation will be known to the statute books, that of total and absolute exclusion of all and every article fabricated or produced, of which the nation in question can make or rear. Until that day arrives, the nations of the world will struggle to undersell and overreach each other ; and one portion, the active, the free, the skilful, will grow rich and absorb all the capital of the world ; and the ignonorant, the indolent, the badly governed, and the weak powers, will stand exhausted to such a degree, that at last, from very necessity, they will have to wake up and supply themselves. The two extremes of rich and poor nations, or of equal powers in these respects, will all work to the same point, that of supplying themselves ; the one from policy, the other from necessity. In the rapid develop-

ments now going on, the time is not very distant
when all this will be verified.   We have now
tumbled in a hurried way through and among the
nations of the world, and taken a rapid birdseye
view of their situation and resources, and seen
plainly enough that they are rich and comfortable
and independent exactly in proportion to the extent that they have cultivated manufactures, and
their handmaid commerce.   We have seen how
necessary a good government, free institutions, enlightened statesmen, sound and permanent policy,
that go to develope resources, manufacture first
up to the home consumption, and next for all the
world that are foolish enough to receive and consume them, are to the wealth and prosperity of a
people.   We have seen how necessary an active
and well-protected commerce is to give efficiency
to the labor of a people, and secure their profits
from it.   We have seen the two extremes of capital accumulated until the whole world is affected
by it, and a nation purchasing abroad until completely exhausted.   The one that expends its income in buying its supplies will be, and must in
the nature of things be poor.   It has to stand up
with its earnings, be they much or little, and hand
them over to the one that is promptest in supplying
her.   It is surplus money that enriches, and if that
be expended in buying goods or provisions instead
of putting it by as made and realized, there will
be no capital, and we may add no independence.
Poverty is the eternal portion of such short-sighted

nations. We will here stop to remark that, in reference to capital, there are three distinct grades of nations. One, like England, eternally adding to her capital by the wise policy of buying nothing but raw materials or tropical luxuries, and selling millions of her goods, and who has got rich enough under it almost to buy the world. Another class, as the United States, has an income that would enrich her, but, for the want of a wise policy, has to lay it out annually to buy the articles of necessity and luxury that she does not make, and will never accumulate capital, but be always snug and always poor. Another class, too low to excite any feeling but pity, that has no income to buy with, and is only half furnished at home. Spain comes under this, and not only does not accumulate capital, but is all the time deteriorating and going backward.

There are, however, other modes of accumulating wealth (not capital). A nation even when she expends all her monied capital in purchasing supplies, is realizing something in the shape of improvements. This is the result of labor exerted at home. The United States, for instance, have made canals, roads, steamboats, towns and cities, new farms, founded institutions, and a thousand things that are the result of labor, yet not in the shape of available capital or actual accumulations of money. The very interchanges of labor effect much of this sort of realization, for houses are built by the exchange of labor between the different mechanics concerned, as masons, carpenters, lumbermen, painters, smiths, and sometimes the farmer.   Roads, canals, bridges, and such improvements, are the work of joint labor, or stock companies.   Books are printed, clothes made, tools, and many permanent fixings got up by a mutual operation of mechanics and farmers.   Were it not for this kind of realization, things in such a country could not be kept up.   It is meeting the natural wear and tear of time, and making and constructing such things as a natural increase of population requires for its accommodation.

CHAPTER XXII.

POOR LAWS.

THE poor laws are a subject of deep interest to political economists.   All writers now are agreed, and experience proves the fact, that poor rates create pauperism—that this eating moth is fed by these laws, and knows no limit but the fund set apart for its support.   I have showed, in preceding chapters, that even in England the poor have been hatched into existence by the poor laws and poor rates.   These rates are the boxes prepared, and the swallows are sure to fill and occupy them to the last hole.   The moment that portion of mankind naturally worthless, indolent, low spirit-

ed, and inefficient, find that they can live without
labor, they will do it. The moment an individual
is base and mean enough to beg, or avail himself of
public charity, unless in the shape of a hospital, he
is totally worthless, and sunk beyond all remedy.
There is no foundation in his case left upon which
to build him up, no pride, no self-esteem, no ambition—in short, the person is not a man, but sunk to
the level of the brute; not a biting, or venomous
brute, but a mere eating brute. Humanity aside,
it would be to the interest of society to kill off all
such drones, get rid of such excrescences, and cast
off such burthens. No religion, no Howard, no
helping hand, can raise them one single step in
the scale of value and availability. The worst is,
that such of that class and calibre as have any
property by accident, or by occasionally working,
instead of taking care of it, forthwith spend it and
frolic on it until gone, knowing that they can lean
on the public charity and find a certainty of support. All providence, all inducement to industry,
and virtue, and economy, are lost and of no avail
in such cases, and with such people. The certainty of getting a tolerable support from the public
destroys all exertion, all providence. Dissipation,
and particularly drink, has brought hosts of such
people to the poor-houses. Had life and existence
depended on their working and saving, they would,
under these last and most operative stimulants have
done it; but as they have the guarantee of a cer-

tainty of support in the poor rates, they spin not, toil not.

It is a very great and important point, therefore, in political economy, to know what remedy to apply to this ulcer, this eating cancer of society. There is but one possible remedy; that is, leave all healthy able-bodied persons to their own exertions, at all hazards. Seeing no provision ahead, all mankind will make an exertion, all will get along, and a great deal better than they do now. Better, if it comes to the worst, let a few perish in the streets, than have one-twentieth part of mankind degraded, rendered worthless, and what is worse, eating the substance of the industrious and valuable portion of the community. Every country could get over the loss of one-twentieth part of its population if an earthquake swept them off, and would soon recover from it; but to have one-twentieth not only lost, but fastened upon it as an eternal eating moth, is infinitely worse. It is not only that portion that is lost but as much more, because it eats its own bulk into the remaining portion of the population. I will venture an assertion that even England would have had no paupers worth talking about, if she had not thus created them by her own poor-rates. All her population now, without poor-rates, would manifest some providence and industry; and the thousands of men, women, and children, who spend all their money, their character and reputation at the gin-shops, would have had no existence scarcely. What a degrading and lamentable idea, yet true, that eight millions of pounds have in one year been raised in England for the poor, which, if taken backwards and forwards, amounts to the damning fact, that that much is taxed on the industry and substance of England, to support gin-shops, gambling establishments, and brothels! This sort of dissipation led to it, and created the necessity for it. It behooves every young country, particularly the United States, after seeing the effect of this system, and the mathematical certainty with which it fills its lists, to pause and take the bull by the horns. Our political economists ought to show this thing in its true colors, and our politicians ought immediately, in all the states, to repeal the poor-laws, and put a stop for ever to the growing evil. Why put our shoulders to burthens that have almost weighed down England, an older and much richer country? We are acting now with our eyes open; for all writers, all statesmen, and every enlightened citizen, see and admit the ruinous tendency of these poor-laws and poor-rates. Let us have some well-regulated infirmaries only for the sick and disabled, and throw upon his or her own resources every healthy person. There is no danger of any meritorious person suffering, or dying for want, in this plentiful country. If some die from dissipation and drunkenness, the community is well rid of them, particularly after habits become confirmed. Religion and a false humanity have conspired in keeping up the poor-laws, and have defeated in it their very purpose, that of saving mankind, for they have made thousands worthless by the very operation. There is nothing like young countries starting right in these respects, because it is hard to get rid of any system after it becomes fastened on them and a part of their annual arrangements. I fear in this country demagogism has much to do with the poor-laws and rates. The poor in some of the states have votes, and their cracked voice is heard in the elections directly. When this is not the case, there is an indirect influence exerted, because the office-holders like to levy and disburse the large funds raised for the poor; it gives them consequence and patronage, as well as emolument. The poor-lists are swelled by such unworthy feelings, and the danger is that the system will be fastened upon us. The poor-rates will increase faster in this country than in England for the above reasons; all this interest and all this machinery contributing to it. These same demagogical feelings in regard to the poor, build for them palaces, and provide so well for them, that it positively operates as a reward for vagrancy, a bounty to laziness and vice. The poor live better, are clad better, kept warmer, more pampered, petted, and thought of, than the industrious poor who support themselves. You pass Philadelphia and New-York, and turn aside to examine some large buildings, looking like palaces or some great national institutions, and find yourself in the midst of three or four thousand gay, roystering,

laughing, lounging, well-dressed rascals, who seem
not to know, or to forget, that there is care on the
face of the earth. You tax your imagination to
conjecture for what great purpose or for what
great merit they are cherished ; and what is your
surprise, when told that they have not fought for
their country, not devoted themselves to religion,
nor are gathered together to work some factory,
and produce wealth—that they are paupers ! You
hear a big bell ring soon, and go in with the crowd
to a feast, a long table set out with viands, better
than a farmer, after all his industry, has to feast
upon. Your ears are stunned with reproaches and
complaints against the beef, the white bread, and
all the laughing potatoes and vegetables that are
loading the table, yet not satisfactory to these lazy
lords. You inquire what Stephen Girard has built
this house and spread all this table, by a donation
of millions of money—for the whole cost millions—
and are still more surprised when told that all
these millions are raised by taxes upon the industry and substance of the land, to support these
worthless and pampered people. You turn away,
asking yourself the question, What claims can
these people have on the industry of the country ?
If they have any, all others may have the same,
and where is the thing to end ? You say this sort
of bounty to laziness is sure to produce all possible
effect.

CHAPTER XXIII.

SLAVERY.

SLAVERY, as it now exists in the United States, is calculated to exert a great influence upon our policy and future prosperity. I am not going to discuss the horrors of slavery, its moral turpitude, nor whether it is right or not. On all these points there can be but one opinion, if the thing had to be gone over again. I merely take it as it exists, as it stands marked and fastened upon us, and intend to show the bearing it has upon our labor, markets, and productions. It is a subject for the inquiry of our political economists, before they adopt any great measures intended to affect our labor, productions, and resources. A new and peculiar sort of labor is through slavery thrown into the United States, that is hard to calculate, and of which the effects are difficult to estimate. Three millions of people or laborers, whose wages are what they eat and wear only, working under other stimulants than their interests, and showing a steadiness and unchangeableness unknown to labor generally, cannot fail to produce such results as could not be appreciated by any rules of a Smith.

These laborers insure and perpetuate themselves, and are guaranteed to the country and their immediate owners by the most sacred and fundamental laws of the nation. No free labor can compete with them, for free labor must have wages that will bear the irregularities incident to all labor, such as occasional relaxation, illness, whims, changes, and dissipations. The free laborers are in families, and useless mouths are to be fed, houses, rents, furniture, taxes, doctors' bills, all amounting to some style and a considerable amount, have to be sustained. The slaves live without beds or houses worth so calling, or family cares, or luxuries, or parade, or show; have no relaxations, or whims, or frolics, or dissipations; instead of sun to sun in their hours, are worked from daylight till nine o'clock at night. Where the free man or laborer would require one hundred dollars a year for food and clothing alone, the slave can be supported for twenty dollars a year, and often is. This makes the wages of the one forty cents a day, of the other six cents only. I prove this by the facts of the case. The average wages or price of labor in the United States is forty cents a day; in England, two shillings, and on the continent of Europe is about twenty-five cents. As far as minute inquiries go, the above rates are correct. A slave consumes in meat two hundred pounds of bacon or pork, costing, in Kentucky, Ohio, Indiana, Illinois, Missouri, Tennessee, and Western Virginia, $8; thirteen bushels of Indian corn, costing $2 : this makes up his food. Now for salt and medicines add $1, and it runs thus : a year's food is $11. Their clothing is of cottons—fifteen yards Lowell, $1 50; ten yards linsey, $4 ; one blanket, $2; one pair of shoes, $1—making $7 50. Now this sum of $18 50, say $20, divided among the working days, is six cents. This is not fancy, but every day's practice. So the wages of a slave is one-sixth part of the wages of free laborers. If slave labor, therefore, was organized to the best advantage, no free labor could stand against it. I have shown before how well fitted slaves are for manufactories, and how confidential and trusty.

The staples produced in this country by slaves, say cotton, sugar, rice, tobacco, and hemp, that would have had no existence without them, for the last fifty years, have averaged fifty million dollars a year, which, in the fifty years, amounts to the enormous sum of twenty-five hundred millions. This sum has been realized, and constituted nearly the whole of our ability with which to purchase supplies abroad. Foreign nations, England more than all the others, have got, enjoyed, and realized, in the shape of capital, this twenty-five hundred million dollars, and we have consumed it, and not a vestige of it left behind. Had we not possessed this resource, we would have been infinitely better off; and, instead of three millions of slaves being fastened upon us, we would have had free people in their place, not growing these staples, but supporting themselves, and adding real wealth to the country, instead of a mere capacity to consume and thereby enrich foreigners. But for this ability arising from slave labor, enabling us to buy so much abroad, we would have been forced by the necessity of the case to supply ourselves, and thus not only have established manufactures, but developed the real resources and independence of the country. We would have been by this time so far advanced in skill and capital that, with our intelligence, industry, and enterprise, aided by an active commerce giving full and efficient effect to them, we might and would have been a wealthy nation, and been now supplying much of the world with articles of our industry, skill, and taste. This people never would have remained inefficient had they not been flattered and lulled by the proceeds of this slave labor. It employed our shipping and commerce so much that, by the aid of our merchants, the slaveholders have governed the country, and kept back every other great interest. The country is now, or will be, in a situation like an annuitant, who, depending literally on the annuity, finds, by some revolution, that suddenly stopped. When slavery shall have run itself out, or yielded to the changes and ameliorations of the times, the owners and all dependent upon it will stand appalled and prostrate, as the sot whose liquor has been withheld, and nothing but the bad and worthless habit left to remind the country of its ruinous effects. The political economist, as well as all wise statesmen in this country, cannot think of any measure going to discharge slavery, that would not be a worse state than its existence. They must therefore pass all laws necessary to control it, render it harmless as to outbreaks and violence, and, if possible, make an efficient labor for the prosperity of the country. They cannot push any farther the staples on an overloaded and clogged market, and should, by inducements, divert a portion of this slave labor from them and into manufactures. There it would begin to count to the country, and through it not only the home supply be made, but a surplus convertible into capital or money. Results that would astonish the world might be produced by turning in the surplus slaves to manufactures, without diminishing one iota our staple productions. We have already proved, in a former chapter, that three hundred thousand slaves might be taken from agriculture and the staples, to their relief, and applied to machinery. This amount of labor, on the scale that England and this country work up to, could produce two hundred million dollars annually. Their productions in this line would find a market abroad from their cheapness, because the character of the labor would be so efficient, and cost only one-sixth of what other labor standing on regular wages would require. I repeat, then, that slavery and its labor enter deeply into all projects relating to the wealth, advancement, and development of this nation, and should be regarded by our political economists as a powerful ingredient.

CHAPTER XXIV

LABOR, WAGES, PROFITS.

ADAM SMITH and the early writers on political economy consider truly labor and its wages as the key to all wealth and human availability. They took it for granted that the wages of labor in all countries tended to find its level and maintain an equilibrium in all departments or employments, and that any bounty made the products of labor permanently dearer by that much. They did not conceive of facts now abundantly proved, that whole departments of labor, or occupations where an expensive outlay for machinery is necessary, remain whole ages untouched without some protection or bounty, and that individual labor enters them not for the reasons given in a former chapter. They did not know the fact that bounty or protection induces so much skill and competition that the goods soon become cheaper than others in proportion, and more than pay back the bounty. Convinced as they were, they necessarily were the advocates of free trade, and against all restrictions.

In former times, when the hands and some simple tools or fixings performed all the operations, and labor-saving machinery scarcely existed, the wages of labor entered deeply into all calculations, and produced great results. Now, when machinery does almost all the work, and requiring only some skill to direct it, no matter how weak and delicate the hands may be, the ground is materially changed. Mankind, as to labor and its wages, stand so nearly upon the same level that the difference is hardly appreciable. The new nations, where labor is scarce and somewhat dearer, generally make it up in the greater fertility of soil, plenty of provisions, the possession of the raw material, and having few debts or taxes to pay. They are more enterprising in their character also, spring quicker into new and promising occupations, and have more versatility in their pursuits. They can afford to risk more than old nations, because they have more recuperative energy and can sooner recover from loss. Old nations are weighed down with paupers, tithes, aristocracy, debts, and taxes, all of which circumstances do nearly make up for any apparent difference in wages. The high vantage ground that capital, machinery, skill, organization, and the possession of all the commercial agents and facilities give to a nation, has not been estimated high enough by those writers that go against restriction, protection, and bounties. It did not enter into A. Smith's ideas that any nation could keep those advantages under the operation of a free trade; and that the equili-

brium the wages of labor tends to would be inadequate to countervail and equalize them. Experience now speaks, and the policy of nations must
regard its voice. Abstractions and theories go
along in a straightforward way, and do not enough
regard the circumstances of nations to conform to
their peculiarities, and profit by their actual condition as to capital and skill. This single fact,
which we now consider proved, that is, that nations which have the vantage ground and start will
keep it, seems to render half the reasoning of these
writers of no practical use. All they say is in favor
of free trade and against restrictions. This broad
principle knocked away from under them leaves
the most beautiful part of their fabric without
support, and lets it tumble to the ground. Instead
of nations tending to the principles of free trade,
they evidently look to total exclusion. I regard,
then, all nations as nearly equal in this respect.
Young nations commit one very common error,
that of leaning on the provision and raw material
culture, and depending on selling enough abroad
to buy their fine manufactured articles, thereby
losing all the wide difference between the raw and
wrought values of things. This gives to them a
hand-and-mouth existence, consuming, annually,
their productions, and realizing nothing in the
shape of capital or money. If they had set out by
supplying their own consumption, and bought nothing from abroad—even if they had sold but little
or less raw material to foreign countries—they

would have been accumulating all the time, and gradually realizing available capital in the shape of money. The people who live in an old nation, where every ground is preoccupied, and no changes from father to son in their pursuits, are less enterprising, because they are afraid to risk any thing; any loss would not only jeopardize but ruin them, and lead to suffering. They cannot turn to other things or employments like a young, versatile people. Success is life or death with them, bread or starvation, and they stick to old forms, old machinery, and work to a disadvantage; which considerations make up still more the difference in wages. It is not difference in wages that determines nations to one or another course, but the circumstances. Young nations, by having fertile lands, and abundance of provisions, and raw materials, lean on them, and go to exporting them as their resources. Old nations, having exhausted these resources, and finding the work of their hands in the shape of manufactures more available, and ready sale, go on increasing until they grow rich. Other nations, becoming scathed by superstition and despotism, and without any guarantee or security for their labor, sink into a semi-barbarous state, do no more than the first necessity of life absolutely requires of them, and stand in the way of no other nations, neither as producers nor consumers.

There are two distinct sorts of laborers; the one on their own account, and with their own hands or simple tools, and may be called manipulators, and own or enjoy all the profits; the others working under capital and capitalists, and are hirelings by the day only, without having any share of the profits beyond their wages. The wages in the one case are merged in the profits, in the other stand clear, by the day, week, month, or year. Competition reduces, very often, the wages of hirelings down to mere support, or food and clothing; then it stands on the same footing or principle of slave labor, only is more wasteful, less controllable, and becomes dissipated and reckless when poor-rates are within its reach, on which to lean and depend. In regard to his own interest, there is nothing creative in the daily wages of the hireling who knows his limit and has no hopes beyond it. The manipulator, or handicraft manufacturer, on the contrary, is all the time creating and giving value to his labor, which he realizes as profit. In all countries do we find the handicraft occupations first in starting and subserving a country; partly because capital is not necessary to them, but more because all the profit goes to the laborer. This class of laborers often realize much, and lay up, money; hirelings hardly ever do realize for themselves, and generally live up to their wages, leaving all the profits to the capitalist. It makes rather a gloomy picture when we say that the tendency of things the world over is, that the competition in labor will bring down all wages to bare subsistence and support, and this with more certainty as machinery becomes more perfect and is applied to almost every purpose. In nations without capital the handicrafts are always first to start and do well, because the prices of the things they make have but little control on the laborer, who sees his labor creating a value where there was none or but little before; and be that value much or little, it is his own, and he can afford it at the market price, whatever that be. Wages, then, may realize capital or may not, according to circumstances, for the laborer; but must be realizing for the capitalists all the time, or the whole operations cease. The elements of wages, then, are subsistence first, which must be had in all cases, and profits next, which must accrue to the capitalists and the handicrafts, or they cease to operate. The handicraft laborers have the advantage of scattering themselves through all countries among the consumers, and can by barter accomplish much. A farmer often will buy an article when he can pay for it in provisions, when he would not without; for then all is completed, and none of the contingencies of the markets encountered. The value of such small interchanges is much greater and of more consequence than they get credit for. It is on this principle that you see shoemakers, carpenters, brick and stone masons, blacksmiths, tailors, millwrights, wagon-makers, cabinet-makers, and all such useful handicraft trades mixed all through the country, and among the farmers, mutually bartering and interchanging their labors. The great question which must ultimately come home to man, as to whether machinery ought to be employed or not, cannot be entertained or discussed, only of such countries as China or Japan, where labor teems enough to do all the work of machinery, and even of beasts, so as to completely banish both, and where they count not upon, and live without, the trade and commerce of other nations. If nations stood alone, like China or Japan, with their full and ultimate population, and a large portion suffering for very subsistence, then it would be better to banish machinery, and even horses, and avail of hand-labor, lest a portion of food necessary to human sustenance be consumed by quadrupeds; accordingly those two nations have done so. Europe, connected by commerce and struggling in full competition, dare not do it; because the nation that first did it would be thrown out of all the markets. From the foregoing remarks there is not much advantage in a nation having a dense population and surplus labor in manufacturing, provided a sufficient number of hands be found to attend machinery. We should not refrain from the establishment of manufactories fearful of wanting laborers: present the handles of machinery, and a plenty of hands will be found to take hold of them, and not only meet our own supply, but the foreign.

Labor is much more efficient in some countries than in others. We have already remarked on the great action our climate gives to us, and that we show it in the management of ships, farming movements, manipulations, and in manufacturing. Our intelligence and free institutions, it has been said, count us largely in our operations, as well as all the advantages of having the raw material, the consuming market, and the great abundance of provisions. Small advantages count, and I will mention that Protestant countries find in the year thirty more days in which to labor than the Catholics, taking into the estimate that number of festivals and holy-days more than the Protestants keep. This is no small difference, and would make up the profits of laborers, and, other advantages being equal, be sure to carry the market, and stand them on the vantage ground. Connected with this is the greater degree of ignorance in which superstitious people are immersed, throwing them still further, relatively, in the back-ground. In times when competition is full, commerce open, and markets, like mistresses, to be won by skill, small advantages and savings count. There are national habits that bear directly on wages. The people of some nations become accustomed to privations, have few wants, and get along all the time without excitement or ambition. In such nations wages are low, and kept so all the time; a little money goes with such a great way, and they, content to live in a hand-and-mouth way, never accumulate capital, often stop work and spend it when in hand. The Italians and Grecians would be examples of such people. In such countries, although wages are low they do not profit by it, for the want of energy, industry, and ambition; and are generally outstripped by bolder nations, where wages are higher, and the mass of laborers feel the force of the excitement of the accumulation of capital. Sterility of soil makes it necessary for a people to be moral, industrious, and economical, and therefore fits them admirably for successful manufacturers. The soil denying to them a profit, they naturally betake themselves to fabrications and creations of their own industry. The steadiness and high confidential character that their morality gives them, the shrewd shifty cunning imparted by their limited circumstances, the privations they are accustomed to, and the few wants they have, render them irresistible as manufacturers, and their savings and profits accumulate wealth and capital rapidly. They soon are known and felt in whatever market they enter, and their goods generally preferred, for their character is necessary to their continued success. The Yankees and Swiss are illustrations of these remarks; and, from their barren rocks and mountains, are putting large portions of the world under contribution. Confined countries force their people also into successful manufacturers, on a principle somewhat similar. No room for agriculture—they are obliged to betake themselves to trade and manufacturing; and, after starting, go on, as Tyre and Sidon of old, and Hamburgh, Bremen, Frankfort, Venice and Genoa, in modern times, and furnish striking examples. All the instances that we have given, prove that the operations of mankind and nations

are very much dependent on circumstances, and
confirm the great principle or rule that we set out
upon, that all political economy is the creation of
circumstances, and whoever undertakes to direct
a nation or a people, of course must closely regard
their circumstances. We see, therefore, without at
all calling in question the abstract principles and
truths in relation to wages, labor, profits, and capital, that they depend very much on circumstances.
Wages are high or low, accordingly as labor is
well or badly employed. We can in all cases,
without Adam Smith, or Mr. Jay, see at a
glance, when we understand the condition of the
markets, the raw materials, the wants of the country, and the amount of its capital, what is wanted
to give effect to and secure the profits of labor.
We see that labor may earn something or nothing
beyond bare support; that it often goes to work
from its own impulses; is very generally governed
by the circumstances in which it is placed, but
often needs the protection and inducements of
governments to go to work rightly and profitably,
especially when working with machinery and under capitalists; and that the ultimate tendency of
all labor in these times of perfect machinery is to
minimum wages, and a lean support. We see also
that there is but little difference in the labor of all
countries, when the wages, quality, and all other
circumstances are brought in and estimated; and
that nations need not, or ought not, to govern themselves by any seeming difference in wages, but

effectuate, regardless of that, any plans they may have requiring the employment of labor.

Most of the realization that is secured and enjoyed in all countries is the result, either of labor when producing no direct wages, or from the growth of countries. As we remarked, the labor of man in the ordinary routine of society, builds up cities, farms, houses, roads, canals, bridges, tools, ships, boats, and a thousand things that are wealth and show an advance, without any money accumulation, or active capital. Again, the advance of population and wants in all countries, make the lands valuable. Whole quarters of cities and villages, and dense settlements, grow upon the lazy accidental landholders; and as in the case of the Marquis of Westminster and others, they wake up to lordly wealth. I could number half a million of substantial farmers in the United States, East and West, who became men of substance by the growth of the country around them, lands rising from a quarter dollar an acre up to sixty, whilst they were in the mean time struggling with an overloaded market, and making nothing but a bare support on their farms. There is every difference in the availability of wealth, whether it be in this shape, or accumulated monied capital. It takes money, detached, hoarded and accumulated capital, to stir up new lines of business, put labor to work, and build machinery and factories. The country, on any emergency, looks not to the houses and farms for immediate relief, but to the monied capital. A people may advance, become in one sense wealthy, and have almost no money. They may become very snug and comfortable by interchanging their labor, and working in manufacturing up to the home market, if that be secured to them. To accumulate monied capital, however, as a nation, something foreign, either in the shape of an active commerce, or exporting large quantities of raw materials, provisions, or goods, seems necessary, and that under circumstances to have the balance in her favor.

CHAPTER XXV.

WAR AND TAXATION.

WAR is a very exciting, though rather an accidental thing. It throws a people on their resources, sharpens their wits, produces cases that show what is necessary, speaks often in the imperative mood, and says certain things must be done. We are a striking example of this. In our late war with England, we began it without the common necessaries of life, much less of war. We made our arms and cannon, our powder and munitions, our common cotton and woollen goods; some blankets, flannels, salt, iron, and many things that now are in successful train from that impulse. Nothing that we then began to make has disappeared, but all have gone ahead, and many of them into full rivalry with England. Until that war we did not think of manufactures, and but for it, and the difficulties that led to it, we would have been, doubtless, servile customers fifty years longer of England. That war has been worth one thousand million dollars to us, and will be worth, in the run of time, incalculably more. Our independence dates as much, or ought to do so, from it, as from the Revolution. The Revolution did not make us free, because we were free before; it merely set us to digging the soil and building ships. We were as much bound to England after the Revolution as before, because dependent on her for all our necessaries and luxuries. The last war taught us to make these things, and now we are free indeed; and now we understand the meaning of the term independence. In Europe, war has frequently stirred up nations to great and capital efforts, and placed them on new grounds, and their whole industry and resources on totally different footings. The wars with Spain and Holland made England a manufacturing and commercial people. The wars waged by Germany on Venice, Genoa, and Italy, transferred commerce and manufactures to Flanders and the Hanse Towns. Wars have built up France, Prussia, and many other parts of Europe, and made them independent and rich. Wars waged in the spirit of civilization, as they now are, prostrate nothing—extinguish nothing in the arts or agriculture. On the contrary, a great deal of money is expended, resources cherished, and every thing, even agriculture, stimulated. Lombardy, Belgium, and the Rhenish provinces, the seats of war for two or three centuries, are the best cultivated portions of Europe. The stimulus of war is occasionally necessary to all people. Nations, like individuals, require excitement—need to have their resources tried, their principles tested, and their characters vindicated and brightened. In a long peace a people become rusty, selfish, sluggish, and less spirited. They either degenerate into slothfulness and meanness, or become absorbed in small gains, and show a trafficking, cheating, money-loving, truckling spirit. They want arousing or awakening up to boldness of character, enterprise, generosity, and sentiments of glory and honor. Wars lead to glory; honor is in the train. If the nation be free, it gains many qualities and sentiments necessary to appreciate and secure liberty. Even in a monarchy it lifts the character, and ennobles the feelings so much, that no despotism would be tolerated. In a republic, particularly, every thing is restless and turbulent in times of profound peace.

No country needs a war half as much as these United States. All sorts of party spirit—sentiments of disunion, tariff and anti-tariff, Jeffersonian democracy, Clay conservative declarations, slavery and anti-slavery, abolitionism, and antimasonry, state-rights and federal principles, nullifications

and nationals, general suffrage and property qualifications, and a thousand other feelings, parties, and
principles, are all the time struggling for the mas-
tery, at the expense of the best interests of this
nation, if not its very existence. The national
character is too low to be felt sufficiently to check
and put to rest these diversified interests and turbulent feelings. A war would lift the federal power
out of the very dust where it lies, and give to it a
character, a name, and perhaps a glory that would
cause it to be respected, and impart to the people
some pride in it. Our feelings of patriotism and
love of country are so scattered and divided between the states and the general government, that
they have no force, and scarcely exist. Every day
things get worse, our national sentiments more
weakened, and the nation rendered less efficient.
Our resources are either wasted by neglect, scattered by division, or lying totally undeveloped.
Our manufacturers are not encouraged, our agriculture overloaded, our staples overdone, and our
commerce hobbling on, for the want of rightly understanding its relations and interests. Much of
our capital has left the country to buy what we
ought to make at home, and debts enough owed
abroad to take the remainder, unless we soon
change our policy. Our active statesmen have
turned demagogues, and are serving their own base
purposes by the meanest and most unprincipled
intrigues and corruption, instead of studying the
true policies of the country and carrying them into

effect. Nothing but a war can save us—can brighten our escutcheon, lift us above all this meanness and local feeling, and make and preserve us a nation. I say make, because we really require new-modelling, new characters, new and better feelings, more available principles, a purer patriotism, and more efficient employment of our labor. We have let the rabble into a controlling power by our general suffrage, and allowed the states to cleave down the central or federal government, until its giant limbs lie more enthralled than did Gulliver's. War, besides setting the national feeling aright, would cultivate our resources, and give a final and effectual support to our labor. We would come out of it with renewed energies, sentiments of patriotism, character of glory and honor, and move off as a great nation ought to do under such impulses. Our statesmen, for the nation's sake, ought to encourage a war whenever it can be done consistently with justice and honor, and our political economists feel that through it would be the readiest road to real independence, manufacturing, and commercial wealth. They ought to do every thing but create a war; never avoid one, rather invite it and meet it more than half way. Without glory and a high national character a republic is nothing, and a monarchy a tame and leaden concern.

The monarchies of Europe could much sooner extinguish our republic by leaving us in peace to corrode our own vitals, than by fighting us. We would in a tough war exert an elasticity that would astonish the old world, and impose upon them a respect for our character that would affect the future destiny of the old regimes. Our scattered sympathies would then be collected; not the federal government, but the local hydras would be nullified; not the conservative power of the Union, but the unnatural and illegitimate feelings that our demagogues in times of a long peace have had time to mature and strengthen. A confederation soon commences an action on herself, on her own members, unless a foreign war engages her restless demagogues. All the parts stand out distinctly, and, without amalgamation enough to blend them into harmony, thrust at each other, and cherish the strongest jealousies and bitterest feelings. The local sovereignties, standing fully organized, are ready for prompt action; not like the case where individuals would have to combine, and could be defeated before they matured any plan or concert. A war, attended with national glory, alone can compress and keep in their places these turbulent states, these local, organized, inherent sovereigns, and centre all the conflicting interests into some great focus.

Political economy is much concerned in taxation, and should zealously inquire into the best modes of taxing; the general effect of all or any tax; and must in reference to it have regard to the circumstances of the nation. Taxes are necessary, and should be laid so as not to shock public opinions and prejudices, or bear injuriously upon any interest. As long as a nation imports enough, the best mode of raising a revenue is on imposts; because it operates equally, and is easily and quietly collected, without any thing inquisitorial or offensive in its mode. Whether in the shape of imposts or direct, a tax can discriminate, and aid the best interests of the country, either by avoiding such as require cherishing, or by bearing heavily upon such as are of no great consequence and can better bear it. Until a nation be ready to prohibit, she ought to tax foreign manufactures high, so as to favor any thing of her own production in that way. It is generally bad policy to tax raw materials, or labor in any shape. In time all nations must and will make their own goods at home up to their consumption ; this is a mark that all move up to ; then the tax on imports would necessarily be confined to such things as could not be grown or produced— such as tropical luxuries, or the growth peculiar to some regions only. If these did not furnish revenue enough, and the tax had to come home and fasten upon the operations of the country, it should avoid the laborer and all articles of the first necessity as far as could be done. The ad valorem principle is the fairest on a general scale, but articles of luxury should be singled out for special taxing, as best able to bear it, and less disturbing the industry of the country. Capital ought not to be taxed when it is in the shape of public improvements or vested in manufacturing, because there it is best subserving the ccuntry. When, however, it is on interest, or banking, or in agriculture and speculation, or lands, or foreign stocks, or not in some direct way touching the springs of industry in the great departments named, it is a proper subject of an' ad valorem tax. Whether a national debt is an evil or not depends on circumstances. If it be owned by her own people, and not heavy enough to require the taxing of labor, and the consumption of necessaries, it is no burthen at all ; but if labor has to be taxed, necessaries reached, and the stock be held abroad, it is a serious evil, a millstone about the nation's neck, and a clog on her industry. The English debt, being held at home, its burthen arises from its magnitude, obliging taxes to go upon every branch of industry and consumption to meet its interest. Within the limits above named, a debt is a blessing. It cements and consolidates the fabric of a government, by making the most sordid concerned in its prosperity, and is a stimulus on all the industry and operations. A nation then has been aptly described as giving a mortgage for her good behavior ; and I will add, a pledge and guarantee of her industry. Such a debt comports with patriotism, and stimulates an eternal vigilance over the institutions of the country. When a nation has idle· capital, it is a godsend to have a debt within the above described limits; offering a safe and ready investment, which does not sink, or destroy, or even deaden capital; for in the shape of national stocks it is just as available : can found institutions, endow schools, provide for the widow and orphan,

and, when wanted, turn into machinery and manufactures.

The worst state of a public debt is where its
evidences or stocks are held abroad. It then taxes
the country for the benefit of foreigners, and exhausts, in the rapid way that spending incomes
abroad or buying all we use from abroad does
and will do. We so far are subservient and even
subject to foreigners, unless we resort to the disgraceful course of repudiating it, or refusing to pay
the interest on it, which would be infinitely worse
than the taxation necessary to meet it. Political
economy should avoid that sort of debt that would
bind us abroad; that would be heavy enough to
affect industry in the shape of labor, or necessary
consumption; but rather invite that which would
be held at home; offer investments to capital; and
not add to the burthens enough to be injuriously
felt. Such a debt tends also to fasten and keep
capital in the country, and prevent that wild speculation which capital indulges in, when devoid of
employment at home. A rational view of this subject would correct that slang that demagogical
politicians indulge in, going to denounce all national debt, and preaching up crusades against it.
Many objects of national improvement require
some debts to be incurred, and the nation is greatly
gainer by them, even at the expense of some taxation. Often great interests are thereby developed,
and brought not only into existence, but to a mar-

ket.   Rather than see its population remain in ignorance and uneducated, a nation ought to incur a debt for a general school fund; and rather than be insulted, and have its national character sullied, and its glory extinguished, it ought to go up to the last limit of a bearable debt.   All nations have seen the time, and will see it, when manufactures ought to be not only started, but aided, if necessary, by loans, and a debt or taxation encountered for them. Great caution ought to be observed by political economists in paying off a debt.   Sometimes it would be much better to use money in developing other interests, if any, than in paying off a debt that is not oppressive.   To pay off a debt discourages capitalists, and inclines them to look abroad for more permanent employment of their capital, and there is a risk of losing that much money from the country.   We should not console ourselves with the idea that the interest would be owned here, even if the capital did seek foreign investment. That is not always the case, for capitalists are very apt to follow their money and reside abroad, when it would be there spent.   There is always a wide-spread shock occasioned by paying off a large debt. The thousand investments in favor of the widows, orphans, schools, improvements, manufacturing, or other developments, become disturbed and broken up, and much confusion ensues.   At no one time ought too much to be discharged; not enough to convulse or distract any interest, or drive capital abroad or into wild speculation.   A nation may

check the over production of any one article, should
too much labor and capital incline to go into it, by
a tax on such production over a certain quantity,
or amount, or bulk; on all cotton bales over a
certain number, or the hogsheads of tobacco over
a certain amount, or manufacturing stock over a
certain amount, or any other thing that threatened
either a monopoly or a prostration of the market.
Should a fear be entertained that manufactures
will go too far, and produce distress by their competition, they might be limited to the home supply
by a tax on the exportation of them, or such as
sought a foreign market. Political economy may,
under certain circumstances of a country, wield a
war, a national debt, and taxation, so as to do much
good in building up its character, as well as subserving manufactures, agriculture, and commerce.

CHAPTER XXVI.

EXTENSION OF TERRITORY—TEXAS, OREGON, ETC.

Our political economists should vehemently oppose any further extension of territory. We have
acquired Louisiana and the Floridas, and are now
reaching after Texas, Oregon, and even California.
We have spread the thin texture of our population
already over millions of square miles, until its whole

tenacity is lost, and it has, for many purposes, no efficiency. This extent of country disjoints all of our feelings and interests, and weakens our sympathies with one another. A population must have a certain density to accomplish any great object. We lie too much scattered to be connected by any system of internal improvement ; half of our people are in the mud, and a large portion too remote from markets to reach any. Hunting and drinking take up such, and render them semi-barbarous. Where roads, canals, bridges, and such works, are wanted to be made, there must be a certain density of population to furnish the facilities of labor, and provisions to aid in the works, and insure a dividend by the use of them. Thousands of miles stand a blank therefore, the population too sparse to have any efficiency, or to act promptly or usefully, either in repelling invasions or in aiding each other's schemes and projects.

Adding Texas to this country will not only prolong the existence of slavery, but give to it a new lease, a fresh hold upon the country. As well might you attempt to destroy a monster by feeding it, giving to it a pure air, unshackled limbs, and a free space to move in, as to hope to extinguish slavery by planting it in Texas. The only principle that slavery in this country will wear out under, is that sort of condensation of population which will furnish hireling labor as cheap as the cost of slave labor, and an abundance of it. Is this to be soonest accomplished by condensing

or scattering the population? All now agree, except some enthusiastic abolitionists, that our slaves,
with the eternal mark of degradation upon them,
fixed, both by nature and fact, would be worse off,
more degraded, if possible, and infinitely more immoral and worthless, if made free, than in their
state of slavery; that no fund, not even of the nation, is adequate to the purchasing out the right,
even if the owners were willing; and would, if
done, create a much worse state of things, a perfect clog to that extent, and a loss of their available products. No fund could transport them
across the Atlantic for colonization, or furnish tonnage and rations for such a vast operation. Three
millions of people, not even by the despotism of the
Romans, the Czars of Russia, or Asiatic barbarity,
have ever yet been forced from any country where
they were native, except by extermination. Slavery, then, will remain among us, mix in with the
population in the long run of circumstances, and is
destined to form the stamina of population, particularly in the delta of the Mississippi river. Abolitionism has the cart before the horse in their
preachments:—instead of the slave running away
from his owner, the masters are destined to run
away from the slave, when they no longer yield
any profit, and nothing but responsibility and
trouble to the owners.

A scattered people cannot be collected quick
enough to repel invasions, or to defend other districts.
Their greatest security from an enemy is the diffi-

culty of finding them. None but the active demagogues, that care not for mud and mire, floods or
swamps, can collect them at the polls to vote ; and
they, the voters, knowing no other, throw themselves into such hands. Information, such as would
subserve them, cannot be imparted : the newspapers and journals that reach them are of the very
worst sort ; and it is so hard to apply any system
of schools or education to them, that nothing of the
kind is attempted. The Lancastrian monitorial
plan, with but little expense and great result, can
be applied to people living together in dense settlements and villages, but totally fails to reach our
scattered population. In this sparse state education is aback, improvements are aback, and all
taste and refinement not only has no place with
them, but is sneered at and ridiculed. All the nations of Europe are advancing in the arts, in education, and refinement, because they are teaching
each other, acting continually on each other, and
sharing each other's sympathies. The only knowledge our frontier men have is of the forest and
hunting ; the only activity they boast of is in
scouring the country, overleaping mountains, mud,
and sand plains ; and the only patriotism, such as
they manifest by reading and acting upon the suggestions of some dirty newspaper that finds them
through the corruptions of the mail or the designs
of party. Talk of commerce, they know nothing
about it ; speak of manufactures, they are told that
England manufactures for them ; their agriculture

is corn and pork, and much of that eaten in the coarsest way at home. But for this centrifugal state, our people might have been collected on one third of the space, and stood far advanced in all the improvements; would have been now making their own supplies, and the country snug and independent. Many differences of interest will naturally appertain to a population without any centre of action and standard of value, or concert in their policies. It would be very difficult to reconcile the wide-spread inhabitants of such a disjointed country to one another, and to any plan of improvement or productive industry that could embrace the whole. If wisdom, patriotism, and purity of intention, were invited to act, and found no political opposition, still they would find great difficulty in applying any ameliorating measures to them, any uniform system of commerce, agriculture, or manufactures, that would cover the whole ground, embrace such discordant materials, and gather all into one focus of national usefulness and individual wealth.

Our politicians and our political economists ought to unite in checking this wandering, scattering spirit, that seems to know no limit, that is to be brought up by the great Pacific ocean only, that seeks new countries not on the principle of conquest or national aggrandizement, but merely for the pleasure of wandering over and pitching their tents upon them. When mankind live more concentrated they act beneficially upon each other.

New inventions become property in common, new lines of business leading to profits and wealth are seen by all, copied by all, and a great excitement and ambition take hold of all, and they advance together, stimulating each other, rising with each other, and have each other's sympathy and support. A dense settlement has in its own bosom a thousand facilities for improvements, and the effectuating and carrying out any project or plan that promises well. Taste, refinement, luxury, education, social and moral excellence, the appreciation of character, the accumulation of wealth and capital, the spirit of enterprise, of commerce, improvement in agriculture, in manufacturing, and all the aspirations to comfort, some standing in society, and some name or character for some available acts or operations—all are active in a comfortably dense population; nothing in a scattered, semi-barbarous, and reckless one. The acquisition of Texas would be ruinous, because it would extend and foster slavery, and aid all this scattering inefficiency we speak of. The daily papers and many other publications place Texas on the proper footing—and no more need be said. The Oregon would detach entirely our settlements and defences, by the intervention of one thousand miles of desert and barren mountains. California worse: Canada not worth fighting for; yet we aim at all and each of these regions. From one extremity of the country to the other, from Louisiana to Maine, from Missouri to Cape Hatteras, all ought

⸱to cry out against the acquisition of any more territory, against our disturbing the Indians any more, or pushing them further back in the face of solemn treaties made with them. To show the recklessness and want of calculation that has run with this scattering of our settlements, and acquiring new territory, I will mention one circumstance : The cotton staple bore a high price, and was enriching the cultivators of the article, from 1800 to 1822. They had a permanent estate and price both, if they had seen it; for there was not good soil enough to overdo the market and reduce the price to almost nothing, as it now stands. These very cotton growers, instead of examining the ground and understanding their advantages, clamored for the acquisition, even by force if necessary, of the Cherokee, Creek, Seminole, Choctaw, Chickasaw, Cado, and Quapaw countries, and forced the government to procure all these regions at great expense and inconvenience, furnishing three or four times the amount of the cotton lands, of an infinitely better quality too, and more than doubling the product in a few years. These regions can produce ten times as much cotton as they now do, and will keep the price all the time ground down to minimums. Never was such a suicidal act witnessed before—never did the innate habit of dispersing and scattering show such a strong example of folly, overruling all private interests, and blindly sacrificing millions invested in farms, and many more millions in the future by the fall of the market. The cotton culture never would have been overdone if these tribes had been left in possession of their lands, or only disturbed as the extension of the market required.

A certain density of population is necessary to a liberal consumption of a country, as well as improvements and a valuable production. Mankind act upon each other in reference to their wants, style, luxury, tastes, and the quality of the goods and food that they consume. One family or individual will not be behind another, and will make effort enough to procure whatever is necessary to give them character, or rather prevent them falling behind their neighbors. A pride and ambition walk forth that stimulate them not only to realize wealth, but show some style, some comfort, some taste and refinement. This is what is called the pride of comfort or style, by some writers, and leads to high and valuable consumption. When this habit is formed it must be gratified, and will make uncommon exertions to do it; will produce more, manufacture more, labor more, and be a more efficient, valuable, and high-minded population. When wealth is attained by a people, these habits of a higher and better consumption spring up; and this wealth is not only felt in improving a nation and people, in establishing manufactures and commerce, and a better agriculture, but in the quality of the consumption, the general style of living, and the general taste that spreads abroad. Wealthy nations consume more and stimulate more productions than a poor people, unless these latter take a turn in commerce and manufacturing that creates wealth for them, when they are no longer poor, and have the means to consume fully. Elegance, taste, and refinement, when associated with wealth, stand not in the way of industry—rather increase its productiveness, from the ambition and factitious wants created, and the spirit and pride that must be gratified. Plenty of money, therefore, carries a people on to still greater wealth, and to a high and proud style of living, when dense enough to act on each other, and consume largely, spend freely, and patronize more extensively the tasteful productions of the arts. When new wants spring up, the abundance of money steps forth and puts in train the machinery and the fixings necessary to their gratification, and induces the skill and labor to take hold and produce them. This plenty of money that appertains to dense population gets the people in the habit of not only spending freely, but raises up all prices of things, such as tavern-rates, grain, horses, equipage, furniture, wages, as in England : still it does no harm when they supply themselves; for being all within themselves, is balanced in the rounds, and prices of all graduate to one another. A nation with a great plenty of money, is always ready armed cap-a-pie for any thing that offers, and is continually putting into operation new things, developing new resources of the nation, and, if properly enlightened and free, is foremost in every market, and in all beneficial business. An abundant capital, therefore, is not a check on a nation's industry, but a vast and ready means of placing and keeping her ahead of others, when dense enough to act on each other, and feel each other's stimulus.

CHAPTER XXVII.

BANKS, MONEY COMPANIES, ACCUMULATION OF CAPITAL, BALANCE OF TRADE, &C.

THE policy of making banks and issuing paper money, and increasing artificially the capital of a country, should deeply engage the attention of the political economist. Occasions may occur in young and vigorous countries, where much is necessary to be developed, and of a safe character, that capital might be beneficially increased by factitious issues. These paper dollars appear and execute their great purposes, by starting works and operations that afterwards go on themselves, without continual aid. All issues ought to be convertible into specie to carry confidence; and if, on emergencies, they should fail to represent specie, the nation ought to stand behind them, and make them good in the end, by receiving them for their dues. A bank whose issue was thus guaranteed could not do much mischief, even if it had to wind up. In com-

mercial cities banks do good, as depositories or
centres where capital is collected and placed out
on short loans upon business paper, and give great
activity to business by their daily operations.
Loans by the year, or long enough to base any
annual improvement upon, become jeopardized by
all the changes incident to business; and if runs
be made, the banks have to stop, because they
cannot call in quick enough to meet them. In long
discounts, therefore, banks do more harm than
good, for they induce customers who enter upon
establishments requiring a long time to mature
them, and on the least alarm curtail upon them so
rapidly that the individual has to stop, and very
likely the bank too, to the distraction of the country. The very time, therefore, that the aid of the
banks is most wanted by individuals, in times of
pressure, these banks have to curtail, withdraw
their support, and ipso facto make the pressure
double upon their customers; and, if this be not
done, have to stop specie payments. They stand
then in a situation to do mischief from necessity—
either their customers or themselves must fail in
difficult times, and frequently, in the doubtful struggle, both, and leave the country worse off and
more depressed than if they had never existed.
Paper issued on the credit of a government would
do more good; for that, not claiming to represent
specie, and yet having the government endorsement,
and made receivable for its dues, would stand in
credit in even difficult times, unless too much of it

were thrown out. The works put into operation by bank facilities or government credits remain, and are a part of our wealth; like the scaffolding of a building, which, when knocked away, leaves the work in all its beauty and usefulness to subserve the public. Whether, then, banking be resorted to or not with any favorable result, will depend on circumstances connected with the state of that country, which would require the consideration of the political economist; and the case must be strong and urgent to warrant such institutions as a means of adding to the capital of the country. Banks do good, however, on the principle that Holland, England, and France use them, as mere depositories of specie and bullion, upon which convertible paper is issued, that, from its lightness, favors transportation, travelling, and exchange.

We have shown, in a former chapter, that there are times and occasions in most countries when certain manufactures or branches of agriculture require to be developed for the independence and comfort of that country : at such times the nation ought to step forward with its funds, if it has any, or its credit, if that be available, and make loans or offer bounties to have the article in question produced. This would be in the nature of a factitious currency, or a temporary increase of money. The productions thus brought into existence often reimburse the capital directly; and again, by the increase of productive wealth, made available. All nations have their crises, not only as

to war and the asserting of their liberties, but as
to the developing of their resources; and at such
times, if individual wealth and capital be inadequate, the nation should step forward and do what
the case calls for, and not lose the chance of any
great operation.   If nations would be on the watch
for such crises, avail themselves of them, and secure
the benefits accruing, they might become rich by
such happy strokes of policy.   The nations that do
get the start of the world have embraced many
such operations, and turned all favorable circumstances to account, by stimulating and aiding individuals to realize the advantages offered.   The English history is full of such crises, and the rapid
developments based upon them seen and stimulated
by her vigilant government.

An extreme case may be encountered when it
might do good temporarily to debase the coin and
sink the standard ; I mean the case where a nation
does not make its supply at home, and all its capital
or money is leaving it to buy goods abroad that
ought to be made at home.   To prevent what little
specie they have, which is never much under those
circumstances, leaving the country, they might
debase it, and thus keep it for a while at home.
The citizens of such a country being accustomed
to see its coin buy according to its face, cannot reconcile it to their notions of interest to feel that it
was not buying its usual quantity, and pause to
do things at home as a matter of necessity.   Such
a resort, however, is indicative of a wretched policy

in the country; and, in the nature of a desperate remedy, is temporizing in its character, and merely intended to throw difficulties in the way of a false and ruinous business. Rather than leave every department of industry undeveloped, and without capital to stimulate them, a country had better risk something in banks, factitious issues, government credits, or loans, and even debase the coin, than stand aback so many years and be utterly impoverished. In the great race now going on in the world for the high prizes that labor and the arts hold forth, every thing should be brought in that could aid in the start and contribute to win some of the prizes. When a balk is made at the start off, a nation scarcely ever again recovers its energies for another attempt, and quietly yields the palm to her fleeter and prompter rivals. Art is resorted to, and often equalizes cases among individuals as well as nations; and why not resort to it, to make up any deficiency of capital in a nation? Money is nothing but a representative value, and why not put out or create enough of these tokens of value to do all that is wanted towards a vigorous start? It might not do to repeat and loan more than once such factitious means in the same operation, for then a want of confidence and a depreciation would defeat the effort. There is a tendency in the trade of a country to conform to any standard of value that is put out. Every thing shapes to it, and all prices quadrate, so that at home it makes no difference in the rounds; and if a nation bought nothing abroad it would matter but little to her what her standard value of money was stamped with. Japan, that has no intercourse with the world, need not care what her coin is, or what value it represents. It is in our trade or intercourse with foreign nations only that a base medium is felt; and whether there be a disadvantage or not depends, as we have said, on circumstances.

Money or capital, most writers say, will find its level and keep up an equilibrium, no matter how much the balance is disturbed. This is not true; and, like a great many sayings that are put down as maxims, needs explanation or exposure. Instead of money rushing into the bosom of poverty, or into the coffers of poor nations, it avoids them, for the best reason in the world—because they offer no inducements, have nothing to sell or buy the money with. It avoids them on the principle that upstart wealth would the poor—not because they stink, but that they have no use for them, or congeniality with them. Where labor is most productive there will capital rush, for there it will find not only products to purchase, but a sure basis upon which to make investments. Draw, then, the last dollar from a poor nation to furnish its necessary supplies, and it will scarcely ever see another dollar; for these dollars remain drawn until she changes her policy and makes her labor and resources available, through which to get them back. We have seen balances remain broken for ages, and capital wholly estranged from countries, until their own wants operate on them and induce supplies created at home, after which capital would begin to flow to them again. The wisest nations of Europe have manifested the greatest anxiety when capital or bullion inclines to leave them: England, when her bullion goes to France for corn, for she never expects to see it again, and never does, for she has nothing to sell to France; she replaces it, however, by her tradings with other and more short-sighted nations less advanced in the great policies of trade and industry. If England and France were the only two nations on earth, the latter, by her wines, raw silks, laces, and occasionally corn, would draw every dollar from England, because she does sell these things to England and buys nothing. Small balances of trade in favor of a nation would, in the long run, enrich her, and exhaust the country against which they stand, had they not, in their turn, some equipoising balances against other nations. Capital finds a thousand inducements to go to, and be invested in, rich nations—none in poor ones ; for it not only is in safety, but can realize itself and its profits so rapidly, when wanted at home, through the valuable products and exchanges incident to rich countries. Let nations, therefore, be guarded against letting their capital go out for the purchase of necessary supplies, for then it never returns.

The balance of trade that forms a part of this chapter, is indicative of the poverty and wealth,

and also of the wisdom or folly of nations. These
balances are either continual, or occasional only.
They are continually against us in our trade with
England; they are occasionally against England
in her trade with the continent of Europe, particularly when her corn crop fails. When a nation
finds the balance against her in a fixed way, she
ought to stir herself immediately to change it, and
resort to legislative enactments, if it be necessary,
of the strongest and most determined kind, before
it exhausts too much. We, for instance, ought to
lay a duty on English goods, sufficiently high to
affect the eternal balance of eight or ten millions
that appears annually against us. We might tax
the goods that we are in the habit of taking from
her high enough to stop them, and oblige us either
to make them or take them from nations that did
not show an annual balance against us. Had we
not a scouring trade with other portions of the
world, that brought in some profit, or a balance in
our favor, our trade with England would ruin us
in a few years. It now not only takes our precious
gains elsewhere, but all the spare cash we have
besides, to keep it up. It is an unpleasant idea,
that our active, enterprising whalemen and traders
have to put in requisition all the seas, all the climates, and encounter dangers, disease, and intense
labor, not to enrich us, but to meet this English
balance that is swallowing up all thus raked together, as well as all at home. How rich we might
become under this enterprise, but for this wretched

policy that makes us subservient to England, France, and the old nations of Europe! A wise nation would not let a balance stand against her in any part of the globe, would put a finger on it the moment it occurred, and make some countervailing movement to extinguish it. In estimating the balance of trade an allowance must be made for the profits of the merchants, ships, and agents, that aid in it, and add them on, or deduct them, as circumstances require. In times of a carrying trade, a balance may be sometimes borne, when a people take goods from one nation to another, and thus realize a profit on them; but this profit must be enough to overcome such balance, or it is not worth while. Our merchants, who scour the world for a profit, sneer at the idea of the balances of trade, and call them moonshine; and our wiseacre politicians, taking the cue from them, join in the feeling, and govern their laws and policies accordingly. Time shows this in its true light, and experience could speak if its voice were heard. Had we saved for fifty years the annual balance England enjoyed against us, it would have amounted to five hundred millions, which, realized at home, would have much enriched us, and might have put quite another face on our circumstances. Instead of free trade or any abstract doctrine overcoming balances of trade, they only make them heavier, and wipe them out in the end by insolvencies, or produce that horrid state of indebtedness that in another chapter we have exhibited against this country. Were there now no nation but this country and England in existence, how long would we be able to stand up to the balance against us? Not many years: and we should act as if that were the case, and correct it accordingly, if we understood our own interests.

A question has been started by political economists, whether capital in a few hands or many is most beneficial to a country. When money remains in the hands that made it by long savings, the owner has a miserly feeling, and when he quits his business, is almost sure to become a usurer, and grind down the poor and needy by high interest; then it would do no good. In order to render capital available, it must be induced out of the coffers of the rich, to go into stock companies or banks, and be loaned out for any useful purpose, either in aid of internal improvements, or any great operations of industry that the wants or policies of the nation require. It then gets into the hands of the million, touches a thousand springs of industry, stimulates the productive labor of the country, and gives to it the ability to consume much, as well as produce much. All diffusion of money and increased ability, however, given to a people that buy their supplies abroad, does more harm than good; for then the whole mass into whose hands it has gotten, use up this money in purchasing goods abroad, and more of it goes off than if it had remained in the coffers of the few capitalists that owned it. We furnish the sad case, as noticed in another chapter, of a people who borrowed two hundred millions from England, and scattering it into the hands of the whole population by a pretence of making canals, or railroads, or banking upon it, all, to the last dollar, ran off to Europe for goods, which are consumed and lost forever, and the debt of the two hundred millions fastened upon us and our posterity.

Stock companies, chartered companies, and associated capital, as well as associated labor, are often necessary to develope some great works and make certain great operations, wholly beyond the power and means of individuals to accomplish. Many great interests would either suffer or be left untouched but for such companies or associations, known in law or not, as the case may be. England is full of great works and results from stock companies, as large as her capital is; and France has suffered much and been kept back by her reluctance to go into them, or the want of confidence she has either in them, or in her government. We have done much through stock companies, and much yet remains to be done ; and they are especially beneficial here where capital is so scarce. The members of a stock company, all risking someting, not the whole of their means, can afford to do it, and have each other's counsel, support, and sympathy in the effort, whatever it be, and are more encouraged to go on under small profits. What great or noted work scarcely do you see in England or this country, that is not the result of companies ? You see a road, a canal, a bridge, a church, a school or academy, a large manufactory, and you may be sure they all sprung from company operations. Our political economists or politicians ought then to encourage such companies, grant to them liberal charters, and exempt them from taxes and dues. A nation had better also co-operate with such companies and become a stockholder with them, than to attempt any work themselves; for they are sure to be imposed upon and defrauded, not only in the outlay in constructing the works, but in the management of them. A sort of unworthy feeling exists among the people, that the government is fair game, and can afford to be defrauded.

CHAPTER XXVIII.

POPULATION.

POPULATION, the principles it depends on, what increases it, how it becomes stationary or retrogrades, are important questions for political economists. It is important to have a full and efficient population in all countries, for the defence, wealth, and refinement, that ought to accompany every government or association of the human family. Political economists should steer clear on the one hand of an increase too fast for the comfortable means of support, and of a deterioration that would tend to exhaust or diminish her resources on the other hand, and also of a stationary condition that would stagnate every thing and produce a leaden fixture over the land.   New countries, with an abundance of land, and not a surplus of labor, ought to encourage the increase of population in every way within their reach, both by a native growth and an immigration.   The natural check and limit to an increase of population is the capacity of the earth to support it and feed it.   To this point it tends, and nothing in the end can prevent its reaching this maximum.   Under certain circumstances and feelings this point will be reached sooner than under others; and in certain countries sooner than in certain other countries.   This is owing to the habits of the people.   If they are without any pride of style, and content with bare support of food, and that of the cheapest and most abundant sort, they will condense rapidly, and their natural increase, on the principles that pigs multiply, be great; but if they have this pride of style and comfort they will increase slower, for they will not then marry without a certainty of that style, and a great portion remain unmarried and will contribute nothing to our increase.   The Irish are a striking instance of a people without pride, and who marry and increase on potatoes alone, in any sort of a dirty hovel.   So long, then, as potatoes exist to feed on, will they go on multiplying.   The English, Scotch, French, and Americans, furnish instances of the contrary habit; and they regard as necessary some style and comfort, before they will marry at all. This pride is a wholesome check on an over-grown population tending to suffering, and keeps it within the limits of a comfortable support. A population without pride, or decency, or taste, or capacity to receive improvements, is worse than none, and instead of advancing, a nation becomes a mass of ignorance, anarchy, and disorder, that is preyed upon by the designing, and is in the way of any real advancement for such nation. How will this thing be corrected or prevented? it is asked. I know of no other method than to cherish a proper feeling of pride in a people; give to them the idea that they are not pigs, and that some style, some comfort, and even luxuries, are absolutely necessary to man. If nothing else will accomplish this, let the legislators of a country forbid marriage, unless the parties make a showing of the means of living decently. This can be done by withholding licenses, declaring illegal all marriages without them, and denying to the parents the rights of citizens, and to the offspring the rights of legitimacy, and a penalty might be superadded to insure it. The growth of Ireland, without pride or means of support, is paving the way for great distress, and puts forward a worthless population, that is eating into the substance of the others, and forms a check to all improvements. There is nothing like an early attention to this thing, for after it becomes a habit it is hard to break and correct.

Let a nation beware of any measure that takes

away the rights, and of course the pride and self-esteem, of a large class of the community, as occurred in Ireland in reference to the Catholics, for it is sure to prostrate them into very brutes. The people and their temples sink together into the dust, as in Ireland, where the priests followed and adhered to the mass of the Catholics; and all stand together on the lowest level of humanity. Nothing can raise them, for they have their pastors with them, and like the smaller spirits that sunk with Satan, are content whilst the leaders share their fate. A population without pride cannot be brought to labor effectually, either on the farm or in manufactories. They have no steadiness of purpose, no plans, no responsibility, upon which to act, and enforce an obligation to labor, or do a job of work. The capacity of the earth to sustain population scarcely knows any limit, when you brutalize man, and take from him the pride necessary to an amelioration in his circumstances. If the sort of improvement be made that will control moisture, make at will manure, or apply chemical stimulants to plants, and give to them certainty, every rood will not only sustain its man but its ten men. Experiments show the practicability of fifteen hundred bushels of Irish potatoes to the acre, and, with a certainty, that is the food of forty-five persons for a year, in the last resort. And at that rate the world is not yet the ten-thousandth part up to its capacity to sustain life.

The human family certainly are as distinct in their capacity to improve, as any two things in nature can be. The Caucasian, the Tartar, and the Malay races advance, and improve their social relations and comforts; the Indians, the Negroes, scarcely at all, and seem in some way the woodsmen of nature; never number a population worth comparing to the former races, and never get out of the wilds of nature. They are fierce on the principle that wild animals are, and courageous as a hungry tiger is, but without plan, purpose, or providence. How differently the continent of America stood populated compared to them! There was not even a nucleus of a population upon which to improve on our continent. We had to exterminate the race as we did wild beasts, before we laid the broad foundations of an organized society. Experience proves that the species were not worth preserving. All the efforts of the humane have failed, and continue to fail before the energy of Europeans. The policy, therefore, that so deeply engages many philanthropists, shows only the goodness of the heart, not the results prognosticated. In the present state of our Indians the best is done for them that could be effected, and our political economists had better let it rest upon this last pledge of the nation of lands on the western frontier for them; and merely watch and defend from intrusion the interest thus conceded. A few more years will destroy the game, and then that master necessity, that always must be obeyed or death ensues, will act on them, and show whether there is any thing in them improvable or available.

A curious problem grows out of the relative longevity of this country and Europe. It stands on a difference, as far as facts go to show it, of ten years in favor of Europe; say those fathers of families that die at seventy in Europe do not pass sixty years here. Now, if the parents of sixty years here have as many children as the parents of seventy there, the only difference at any given time in the population of the two countries will be the few persons then living between sixty and seventy years of age, which would not much effect the result. A greater degree of longevity then is not as much in favor of a country's populousness as it might appear at first sight.

Fixed costumes, fixed notions or modes of living, and fixed pretensions, are what ought to be avoided in all countries, if possible. As soon as a people feel that there is no more advancing for them, that they can accomplish nothing more, and have no right to aspire to any thing further, there is an end to all improvement, to all amelioration, and bettering their condition. Such a population becomes leaden, and not only stationary, but ready to fall back, and sink still lower in the scale, if any thing should require it. If mankind do not advance, the next best thing is to have the wish to do so, and the susceptibility to be acted upon by favorable circumstances. There

is some hope of them then, and some foundation
to build on, when occasion calls it into requisition.   Can there be a more dead, really inanimate
state than the castes of Hindostan ? As well might
you operate on dead matter, as to any plan of improvements, as upon such a moral and political
fixedness. Nothing can lift the great weight
above its calculated level; nothing counteract the
vis inertiæ, the mere gravity of the matter.   In
many parts of Europe, the fixed costume and dress
of the peasantry seem to say, here we are, and here
we are destined to remain, and it is folly to aspire
beyond.   In France, and in many parts of Germany, there are fixed costumes in the peasantry,
that indicate their opinions of themselves, and
how devoid of pretensions they are.   When a nation gets ready to advance in manners, circumstances and information, it should find no difficulty
in the fixedness and habits of the people to its progress, for it loses time to change these and prepare
them for the changes.

As nations grow old, if they are well governed,
they grow in comforts too, and are more healthy.
The bills of mortality in England, France, and
Holland, show better than in our country. Fewer
die out of season, and more of course grow old.
England has ameliorated in this respect twenty per
cent. within sixty years. The country becomes
chastened, better drained, drier, better shaded, the
inhabitants better sheltered, housed and lodged,
and warmer clad.   A thousand improvements take

place in their food, transportation, travelling; not so much in the quality of the food as its regularity, and mode of preparing it. Mankind are becoming more temperate in eating and drinking, as well from necessity as principle. When a people are temperate and regular in their diet, have not much variety, and few temptations to indulgence, they will be more healthy. The principal reason of better health, is the purer state of the air, fewer malaria, and miasmata, and less nuisance. There is a state, however, very different from this, when a nation as it advances in population by some bad government, advances also in poverty and wretchedness. Disease walks then abroad among such a population, and strikes down its thousands. The poor wretches rather invite it than avoid it, for it becomes a relief to their miseries. None of the comforts, none of the precautions are prevalent that could either prevent or cure the ill health wretchedness is heir to, but the removal of the very cause of the wretchedness itself, the full sweep of despotism that has produced such misery. Where there are no guarantees of safety for either persons or property, one unrelenting and ruthless tyrant stretching over the whole mass, and urging and oppressing a thousand smaller tyrants, who, to supply the grasping demands, have to oppress in their turn all the wretched population, until all are destitute and paralyzed; what money they have then they hide and make nothing, because rapacity would seize it. This kind of a population is not only utterly worthless and unavailable, but diseased from want, privation, and misery. There is no remedy for such a condition—all is lost, all is brutalized, and could not be reached by any laws or rules of economy, and rendered healthy and efficient, because there is no foundation on which to operate. Where tyranny has no check, property and persons no guarantee, and industry no result, economy can aid naught.

CHAPTER XXIX.

EDUCATION, AND THE PUBLIC LANDS.

The education of a country, and the information of the people ought to engage in the deepest way our political economists as well as our politicians. If knowledge is power, as is properly said, let us make sure of its influence, and implant it firmly in the land. A people are efficient in their daily pursuits exactly in proportion to their information, and a government wise and powerful on the same principle. For no purpose, except the establishment and preservation of liberty, should a people bear taxation so willingly as to raise a literary fund. Our politicians should feel that nothing was done as long as this great field remained uncultivated, as long as any portion of the people remained in ignorance. Education is a national concern, a first duty, and the only true support any free institutions can have, upon which to depend with certainty. These United States should have erected their great landed domain into a fund for the education of the whole mass of the people. Both primary and finishing schools, rudimental foundations and universities, the arts, and agriculture, political economy and religious instruction, could all have rested on this wide basis and found ample funds and support. A course, however, unworthy of such a people with such a fund has been pursued, that threw it all to the four winds, that wasted these sacred means thus intrusted, and has left the great subject of education to chance or to the local authorities. The sticklers for state rights, and the anti-federal or democratic party, have denied to the federal government the power and the right over education ; and, having the control in the councils of the nation, have tied up the hands and defeated the intentions of the general government. Before this influence was asserted and recognized by the American Congress, it had set apart one-sixteenth of all the public lands as a fund for primary schools within the new states where the lands lie. They also gave two townships of land to each new state for a university within the same. This was probably the commencement of a system that by some further plan, had it not been arrested, would have embraced the old states also, that were equally entitled to their part, on every principle of justice, and might have worked much benefit to the great cause of human instruction. This contracted decision, however, occurred and stopped the thing in this partial, unjust, and unfinished state, and lost the only chance of doing the great work and accomplishing such a mighty purpose.

The new states who got this landed fund have wasted it nearly all. They sold the land thus sacredly intrusted to them by virtue of their sovereignty, which felt indignant at the idea of being considered a trustee, even for the benefit of their own people, and have expended the funds accruing therefrom either in ordinary expenses, mad projects of improvement, or in the defalcations of their politicians and demagogues, who advocated the sale and used up the funds as they came into their hands. This landed fund, as partial and unjust as it was, amounted in the new states to ten millions of acres, and might have done much good had it been saved. It would have been sufficient to educate the whole mass of the population in those states for ever. Education now, although of the last importance to all free people, is entirely dependent upon individual and state regulations. Some of the states, to their credit be it said—such as the New England states, New York, New Jersey—have created funds, and all the people within their borders are really now in the act of receiving a proper rudimental education. In the other states scarcely any move has been made in it at all, only as individual settlements and inclinations prompt to it. In all the new states the population is so scattered that no plan of instruction can be successfully applied to them. The Lancastrian monitorial system, as we have said, can only be applied with any benefit to a dense population. Then a little money can collect and educate all, or rather put all in a train to educate one another. A frontier man neither appreciates an education, nor is he in a condition to avail himself of it, if he wished to have his children informed. He has no neighbors, or not enough to share with him the expenses; and, as he cannot do it alone, his children grow up without any, and are content with the knowledge of the gun, the woods, and wild nature, instead thereof. One-third, therefore, of the population remain in ignorance under this chance-medley system, or no system at all, and are a prey to designing politicians or demagogues. There can be no dereliction of duty in a government at all comparable to this total neglect and abandonment of education. As well might we surrender the great principles of liberty, and make up our minds to yield up all the benefit of free institutions; for, without intelligence in the people, all is compromited. It is the first duty of a national government to provide for the education of every individual citizen, so far as the rudiments are concerned, and not rest until it be accomplished. It remained for these wise statesmen to make the discovery, that learning is a dangerous thing in the hands of the Federal Government; and that any system of education might, through it, jeopardize our free institutions. Nothing but the grossest ignorance or the most wicked designs could have arrived at such ultra and unheard-of conclusions. The very existence, the self-preservation of all governments, would imply the power to educate and enlighten the citizens, without any expression in the constitution to that effect, and all good patriots would so take it. This anomalous, this fastidious and crippled government, however, has set the example of totally disclaiming the power, has wasted the great fund that nature seemed to furnish her for the purpose, and now reposes her liberty and her best policy upon accident or local exertions in this respect. A nation should found universities, colleges, and lyceums, as well as the primary schools. She should collect, in connection with them, libraries, apparatus, museums, cabinets, and specimens for all branches of literature. She should also have galleries of paintings, statuary, and all the fine arts; and also models and samples of the useful and mechanic arts, as well as an observatory, botanic gardens, and sample farms. When a nation moves in these very useful and necessary departments of human knowledge, all the citizens lend themselves to them, and make it a part of their ambition, not only to avail of them but to aid in every way within their reach and ability; and they become centres for all valuable collections, and monuments of national pride. When a nation provides funds, there is certainty in the thing, and all the people repose upon the foundations thus laid. A controlling influence is lit up by such intelligence that tempers and directs the great policy of the country, and keeps in bounds those wayward politicians and designing demagogues that often disturb the good order and best interests of society. Political economists should not rest one moment until they place the education of this people upon a national and certain basis. They should cry aloud and cease not until some act of Congress be passed that would give either the remaining public lands for the purposes of general instruction, or create a fund in some other way that would cover the whole ground and fill up this yawning chasm, this blank space, this dangerous vacuum in the public mind.

If they fail to excite this prostrate giant called the Federal Power to action for this purpose, then they should travel down, or rather up, to the constituent sovereignties, the states and city corporations, and urge it upon them, as the only remaining chance of benefiting the people and establishing systems of instruction. The necessity is daily becoming more urgent, since a general suffrage walks forth through the land, and converts almost every male into a voter. A general suffrage without education is sure ruin to any government. It will throw all the available interests of the country into the hands of designing demagogues, and pervert to base and selfish purposes all their resources. Intelligence alone can stay such hands, can say, Este, este, profani !—hence ! touch not the sacred rights of man with polluted hands! So regardless are our citizens of the advantages of education, that when vast funds are devised by humane men for the purpose, they are perverted and wasted, and the best intentions of the deceased not only defeated, but such examples held out that others are deterred from so devising their funds, for fear of abuse. Witness the great Gerard legacy to Philadelphia for education, that has been wasted; and the Smithson legacy to the nation, equally wasted, or loaned out to demagogues in a way either to be lost or not available. In addition to the funds provided for schools and the necessary preparations, there should be some penalty for not using them, and availing of the advantages thus held out. No person should be allowed to vote, or hold office, or serve on juries, that could not read and write; and an invidious tax might also be laid upon such as have property, obliging them to pay more than others: their shame and pride might also be acted upon by setting up in the public places, and having it published also in the journals, a list of the names of such as could not read and write in each county and town. A set of rewards or distinctions of some sort might with advantage be provided for such as distinguish themselves in the primary schools, and such should be singled out and sent up to the colleges or finishing schools at the public expense. A stimulus could thus be given, not only strong enough to carry all into the schools, but to put them upon an effort for the prizes. The Lancastrian monitorial system can be applied with less money and more effect to a dense population than any other, and should be adopted. As far as practicable, too, the Pestalozian or natural method should be tried. The natural signs of ideas, when used, give a rapid and perfect perception of the thing represented. All the physical sciences and many branches of mathematics can be taught, with great saving of time, by specimens, museums, and counters or diagrams. A small expenditure would fill the lecture or school rooms with these aids in the acquisition of ideas. There should be no distinction by separate classing of the poor and rich in the primary schools; the poor scholar, who is educated at the public charge, should not know it, nor the others with whom he studies, lest he be mortified and depressed, and become a butt or mark for the others. Much may be done by night lectures in all cities and dense settlements; and these lecture rooms, and the lecturers, with the proper apparatus and specimens, should be furnished at the expense of the public, and examples set by those in office, and those already learned, to the laborers, to induce them into them. When any system of teaching, well supported by the proper illustrations, takes hold on the laboring population, they will not fail to attend them, and benefit much by them; and these very improving rendezvous take the place of grog-shops, gambling, and all sorts of dissipation.

I think it is entirely practicable to render all

the population, including laborers and operatives, learned, and even scientific, by the aid of night lectures with the proper appliances, without taking them from their daily avocations, or at all interfering with their productive labors. This would present a picture unknown to the world, and realize more than man has ever aspired to or hoped for. Those great capitalists that are moved by their philanthropy enough to leave millions for the purposes of education, and to enlighten the human race, would do well to order lecture rooms to be built in some large cities, and filled with libraries, and apparatus, and specimens; and with a fund to support the necessary number of lectures on the Pestalozian plan, or natural method. They would do infinitely more good with a given sum of money in that way than any other, and build up in the hearts of men a monument that would be more imperishable than marble or brass. Had the Girard fund of three or four millions, for instance, been so directed, it could have planted a lecture room in every square of the city, well furnished, and well filled with the proper lecturers and appliances. Twenty lecture rooms, used every night, would embrace all the population of such a city as Philadelphia and its liberties, and move the whole mass up to science and a respectable information. The ground and a building to hold two thousand persons, would cost, say $10,000. The library, and apparatus, and cabinet of each, would cost, say $20,000; and a fund, out of the interest of which to pay a lecturer $1000, say $20,000, would be for each building, its appliances, and lecturer, $50,000. Twenty such establishments, then, would only require $1,000,000 to be got up in the complete way. Girard's fund, then, would have thus furnished Philadelphia, New York, Boston, and Baltimore, with the means of education in this available way. It would be a good idea and a national policy to set apart a yard or ground near, or at the seat of government, and consecrate it sacredly to the monuments of such benevolent persons as devise their estates, or give their property for the purposes of education, with the appropriate superscriptions commemorative of the deed. Nothing connected with this government is so discouraging to the cause of liberty, and derogates so much from the character for intelligence and high manly feeling and an exalted patriotism, as the discarding all education from the federal government, and throwing it upon chances. Our only appeal now is to the states, and there we meet a supineness and a recklessness in regard to it that puts all aback, or at least postpones it indefinitely.

The public lands or national domain in the United States should engage the attention of our political economists and statesmen. So far they have either been wasted, or formed a subject of controversy in all of our legislation, that has interfered much with all true and patriotic movements. The new states have set up claims continually, not only through their individuals, but as states, that have no regard to justice or equity.   No law can now be passed by Congress, scarcely, that does not involve some question, or some combination, bearing upon the public lands.   As we have said in the preceding chapter, these lands should form a fund for a system of education, primary schools, colleges, and so forth, that would embrace the whole mass of the people.   The fund is ample, and would bring in a revenue of two million dollars annually.   This fund is provided by nature, seemingly, for the very purpose, and would save any further effort, or any burthen of taxation upon the country.   The nation could do very well without this fund for its ordinary wants or revenue, and would have the satisfaction of seeing the great plan of human instruction going on without feeling the weight of its support.   This fund might be erected into a sort of annuity yielding not less than two to three millions, and would insure what is of vital importance to all republics. The temper of this nation would not favor a tax heavy enough to accomplish this great desideratum. A Bureau of Education would sound well in the departments of government, showing its annual results, and setting forth its funds and disbursements. A nation is concerned in having every individual raised from a state of ignorance to one of light and intelligence; to have its voters all citizens, and efficient, instead of brutes and imbeciles; to have men come up to the polls to think and understand and vote on the true independent principles, not be brought up as automatons or brutes by the active and designing demagogues for their own base purposes. The states are setting up claims to the public lands within their dominions, and threaten the seizure of them. This will be done before many more years under our broad state-right feeling, accompanied with a contempt for the federal government. A little more demagogueism will do it, and this fund be gone forever. This nation cannot stay the hands of rapacity when put forth by the sovereign power of a state, but will stand by and see it accomplished without gainsaying it. In the present texture, and under the present feelings of the states, every thing they or any one of them aims at will be acquiesced in. Never will this nation move against a state, because it has no troops scarcely of its own ; and the sympathies of the states will prevent any state either moving against a rebel or rapacious state, or furnishing a quota of militia to help control her. Unless something be done soon with the public lands, they will be lost for all useful or available purposes. The danger is great, and every year becoming more so, of collisions between the federal and state governments ; and these public lands will be that bone of contention, most likely, that will lead to them. It is therefore the duty of our statesmen and political economists to turn them into some useful channel, that all might abstain from disturbing, because all would be benefited. There is nothing of so general an interest, and that could be so happily applied to all, as some just plan of education. The next best use

that could be made of them would be to get up
some extensive plan of internal improvements, as
we shall hereafter show.

CHAPTER XXX.

INTERNAL IMPROVEMENTS, THE MAIL, ETC.

THE great interest of internal improvements,
consisting of canals, rail-roads, common McAdam-
ized roads, bridge s,ports, light-houses, beacons, and
defences, are of national concern, and claim the
attention of all political economists and statesmen.
That a nation should construct forts, and all sorts
of fortifications necessary to its defence, is not denied by any party, not even in this fastidious age.
We have, therefore, made many such works, and
perhaps almost as many as are necessary, or as
we ought to make. We have also gotten up a
corps of engineers and a military academy, with a
bureau of surveys, maps, designs, and admeasure-
ments, of our coast, its depth of water, of our
heights and levels, and every thing relating to the
defences of the country and a right understanding
of its resources. We have also built the proper
number of light-houses, beacons, buoys, and harbors,
for the safety of our commerce and navigation.
We have stopped the good work here, and have
been rudely arrested by a set of politicians, under

the influence of the Jeffersonian Virginia school, who are state-right sticklers, and so construe the federal constitution as to withhold the power of constructing roads, canals, and bridges. It remained for these wiseacres to discover that it would in any way endanger or jeopardize liberty or the great principles of freedom, to construct a road, a canal, or a bridge! Such is the pretence, however, as absurd as it sounds. The constitution expressly gives the power to wage war, establish post-routes, and commerce, to all of which the road making is indispensable, and if not named, would have been necessarily implied; yet these party and unmeaning scruples affect to think differently, and say, because it is not named, it is withheld. Any thing essential to the very existence and preservation of a government, would necessarily run with that government as a part of its vital principle, of its very existence, and requires not to be given or named. So determined now are they in their rigid construction, and so strong in the councils of the nation, that they not only deny the power, but carry out the principle, and either stop or prevent any work of the kind from being done. A few of the states have the funds and wisdom to make such works by their own means, and from the impulses of their own wants; but these are local works, hardly ever national in their character, and lie across the great lines that a nation would move in rather than run with them. New-York, Massachusetts, Pennsylvania, Ohio, and Maryland, particularly, have done wonders in that way, and some of them incurred debts in their zeal too large for them, and are either oppressed or discredited by them. They have been doing the work of the nation, and as far as they go have redeemed much the character of the country in this respect. The other states are in the mud and mire, and have no communications or outlets for their produce, except such as nature has furnished in some places to their hands.

In the last war with England, it cost more to get our armies on the Canada frontier or to New-Orleans than the thing could bear; hence, on the northern frontier, we were never able to collect a force strong enough to take Canada, or even prevent her annoying, burning, and plundering of our whole frontier. Every barrel of flour cost fifty dollars, every barrel of pork eighty dollars, and every cannon used there twice as much in the transportation as the cost of making it. Of the one hundred and sixty millions of dollars which the last war cost the nation, eighty millions were for transportation alone—a sum which would have built rail-roads and canals over the whole space twice over. This nation has paid enough for the transportation of its stores in that war, and before and since, to have checkered the whole country with the finest sort of internal improvements, roads, bridges, and canals; and if we add the tax additional that produce and goods have paid, and had to encounter in getting to and from market, it would have amounted to a sum as large almost as the English debt. The mail now almost daily fails to reach its destination when it goes South or West, because it has to flounder through the mud without either roads or bridges to facilitate its passage. New Orleans, a most important point as to produce and markets, fails to get its mail in winter more than half of the time, frequently whole weeks together, at a time when the price of her valuable staples hang on a variable market. In that market have occurred cases where that city has lost money enough for the want of knowing the real state of the market in time, to have made a road all the way, so as to connect her with the East—say five millions in one season. On the score of a true and regular mail, then, roads are very necessary, indeed almost indispensable. General information should promptly reach every point of the country, as well as the state of the produce and stock markets, and army movements. On our long line of frontier, in case of invasion, we should be able to throw all sorts of supplies and defences to every point with all possible rapidity, as well as the information of an enemy's movements. How can this be done without roads, canals, bridges, and steamboats? What sort of a nation is it that folds its hands, and denies to itself the right and power to do such things, to offer such facilities, to send forward all possible aid, and impart the earliest information? History cannot furnish a parallel case of culpable and shortsighted forbearance. Such politicians must be unworthy guardians of the sacred cause of liberty, of the invaluable principles of freedom.   They deserve to be stricken from their trust, and to lose all the boons that God and nature have given to them.   If we suffer so much in the defences and efficiency of our country in war, and in our mail operations, for the want of these intercommunications, it is still worse in a commercial point of view.   War is only occasionally in want of such things—commerce ever.   A stream of commerce is always wanting to pour its wealth and comforts into the interior, and every day, every hour, encounters these difficulties.

We, like inconsistent beings as we are, go to great expense in inducing a trade or commerce to our strand from abroad, and there leave it to find its ultimate consuming market in the interior as best it can, or not at all in some cases.   Our power ceases at the strand; we cannot aid it further.   The ten millions a year that we expend in inducing it to our strand and accumulating it there, by our naval, harbor, light-house, beacon, and buoy fixings, is worse than lost, unless we render it available after that, and aid it in finding the consumers.   The absurdities of our politics, taking into the estimate our state-right doctrines, anti-tariff operations, anti-improvements, and all the other inconsistencies that eternally envelope us and our policy, are more mysterious than the Egyptian Sphinx or the Delphian Oracle; and the motives that inclined our politicians to such things are entirely inexplicable on any prin-

ciples that ordinarily govern men.   Our pride, our
nationality, patriotism, love of glory and honor,
and even of a rational liberty, seem entirely ex-
tinct, or some very different feelings would seize on
us and direct our policies.   In this age of improvement, of development, and amelioration in every
department of human economy, why do we not
only stand still, but throw back the whole advance
of this nation ?   When the world is educating itself, why are we in ignorance ?   When commerce
envelopes the whole human family, throws around
and among them every variety of comfort, and
every luxury, as well as necessity, why are we
throwing across its currents these chevaux-de-frises
of sand and flood, and bars of every sort ?   When
a creative resource walks forth, and with its sacred
wand touches into life and existence thousands of
values that had been long dormant, why do we stay
the magical and wonderful operations ?   When the
arts all want the aid of some paternal government
to foster and cherish them, why are we a blank ?
When mankind are condensing into villages and
settlements, and not only teaching each other, but
enriching all the social relations, why are we scattering off into the woods and wilds, into Texas,
Oregon, and the far west, and hiding ourselves
from all these social enjoyments and sympathies ?
When manufactures are encouraged the world
over, and every people trying to supply themselves
with the elegancies and comforts of life, and form a
foundation on which to trade and hold intercourse

with all the world, why are we clodhoppers, and
not only suspended in this great field, but dependent upon and slaves to other nations and people
who are more alive to their interests? Why do
we not brighten our escutcheon, hold ourselves
forth as worthy of the liberty intrusted to our
hands, and exhibit a people well instructed, well
clad, well furnished, and proud of their country;
instead of warring upon our own institutions, and
grinding all our character as well as our best interests into the very dust? Go to England: she is a
unit in power, by the facility her roads, canals, and
steamboats give her, and passing rich from her manufactures. Go to France: she is connecting the
two seas that she is contiguous to, by roads, and
canals, and the wine, corn, and manufacturing districts. Go to Germany: the Rhine and the Elbe
are coming together; the Baltic and German seas,
the Adriatic and the Danube, and all are teeming
forth their interchanges and trade, until Germany
is at last really one nation, whether emperors, kings,
or princes govern her. Go even to Russia, where
lately the slave was tracked in his own snows by
his chains only: now the Black and the Baltic seas
are coming together into commercial communion;
the Caspian and the Baltic, the latter and the
White sea; the whole moving in the great work of
intercommunications and commercial thrift, and the
autocrat now playing with railroads instead of human life, and delighting in commerce rather than
human misery and butchery. Why do we stand

with folded arms and look on these mighty movements?

It is for us above all others to be foremost in
the race, in such great facilities. A wise politician
could scarcely conceive of a people, especially one
pretending to more freedom than any others, and
one to whom the very palladium of modern liberty
is intrusted, her very temples consigned, standing
still, and not only seeing all others outstripping her,
but doggedly refusing to move at all. A nation
that, worse than the wagoner who prayed to Her-
cules, neither helps herself nor is asking others to
help her. She sees her lights one after another extinguished or eclipsed by her rivals, for the want of
an equal or proper movement. A chance-medley
people, whose forests shelter them instead of regular
defences; whose instincts serve them instead of light
and information; who associate with wild animals
instead of rational beings; and live without wants,
rather than make and protect the fruits of their labor,
the things necessary to refinement and civilization.
We require rapid movements, we need free and
certain and available intercourse to understand
each other's plans, enjoy each other's society, and
exchange each other's varied and useful products.
Can rational liberty live in the wilds, where belongs only an unrestrained nature?   Can freemen
speak in the boldness of independence, and have
their voices heard, when hid in remote and unhal-
lowed places?   The first lesson I would give to a

free people, to an independent nation, would be to circulate freely, bring every interest and every individual together, and give and receive each other's ideas and sympathies rapidly, and continually. Move in mass, think in concert, and grow strong in each other's sympathies. We have one liberty to defend, one long line of territory to protect and guard, and a very varied commerce to diffuse to every part. Let us then enter on a system of internal improvement in earnest, depart from those illiberal and jealous and confined notions that suspend our very existence as well as prosperity. Let us be a nation worthy of the times, worthy of a free and enterprising people, and show to the world an example of activity, intelligence, and energy, that will call down their admiration upon us, and gain for us our own esteem, and that glory and honor that are more necessary to republicans than any other sort of people. Let us have roads, canals, schools, monuments of the arts, galleries for taste and excellence, and every thing that would not only show us a nation, but preserve us such. It is time the parts had yielded to the whole, the states to the federal government, as far as is necessary to national character and respectability. The states will be in contempt, be in broken and scattered fragments, as soon as the central power be put down. Like the elegant mirror of the parlor, as a whole it reflects all, and multiplies perfect and grand images of the scene, but if dashed by rude hands into fragments, each piece does but reflect some disordered, disjointed view of the grand whole.

As we have said before, unless we could agree to appropriate the landed domain for a great plan of education, the next best thing that we could do with it would be a plan of improvements that would cover all the ground, aid our war defences, our mail transportation, the distribution and diffusion of our commerce, the carrying off of our large agricultural productions, and the bringing us together for mutual instruction and sympathy of feelings, as a people of the same nation. Facilities given to remote settlements to send off their productions, often carry with them a creative power, often give value to what possessed none before, and increase that of all others. A thousand things along the line of railroads or canals, that lay without notice or any value, come forth when touched by this magic wand into being and availability; citizens often get a shaking up from a state of lethargy into which they had fallen, and become actively useful and intelligent. Often the means of doing some good work, founding some useful institutions, are thus awakened and brought forth into use. We feel as if we were in the great world, and an efficient part of it, when we daily are thrown in communication with it, and made to act our parts.

What a beautiful system of roads and canals might have been made in connection with the public lands! Lines of roads and canals might have been pushed into all the new states, and through them in all directions; and after they were finished the lands alongside of these lines would have sold in all cases for as much more than they did as these works cost, and the country thus have had the improvements for nothing. The foresight of political economists would have foreseen it, but that of demagogues never looks to such advantages. The opportunity is lost forever, and the lands wasted, or so much gone as to be inadequate to such a plan for the perfection of which they were susceptible. degrading doctrine of constitutional difficulty, now ties up the fund forever, and holds the hands of this imbecile government. The states have set up a great automaton called the Federal Power, whose limbs are clay and whose force is nothing. Like the Indian's idol, they mock it, and teach other nations also to disregard it, and laugh at its awkward appearance and helpless condition. Nothing can fill up the measure of this nation's destiny but intercommunications that will bring all the parts together, and effectuate that rich commerce that such varied and valuable productions would naturally sustain. Nothing can amalgamate this people, make them united, and their government a unity in its effect, but such facilities.

The post-office department is entitled to all consideration from statesmen and political economists, as bearing upon its wings the information that must concern the whole, and summoning all

to obey the same impulses in danger, and feel the
same interest in the grand routine of daily duties
and daily operations. If a people be highly educated, and intelligent enough to read much, the mail
furnishes the pabulum of this very laudable appetite, and may be regarded as the handmaid of education as well as politics. The presses are teeming now with cheap and useful matter, that ought
to reach every part in the greatest cheapness and
with all possible despatch. Novelty, that seizes
so strongly on the mass of mankind, ought to be
made available whilst the curiosity, the natural
manifestation of it, be active and fresh. Staleness
in reading matter blunts much the appetite for
reading. It is in commerce and politics, however,
that the mail is most important. A free people
should have the freest and most rapid intercourse
with one another; and all the parts, even the most
remote settlements, ought to know what the centre
and every other district is doing, and how they feel
on all subjects and measures. The post is more
important to a free people, to republicans, than to
the inhabitants of a monarchy or of a despotic
government. In the former all correctives must
move from the people; in the latter, they have but
little to do with any operation of the nation, and
it suffices such government to convey orders only
to the subject. There is something vivifying and
exciting in a rapid mail communication to free
people, that keeps alive the full tide of patriotic
feelings, and modifies them as the exigencies of the

country require.   When any thing retards or ob-
structs the mail, there should be a power and a
fund to act immediately and remove the difficulty.
Nothing would argue so much a defect in the policy of a nation, a carelessness in the important arrangements necessary to the efficiency of a government, as a neglect of the mail communications.
This nation is denied, as we have said, the power
of constructing roads, or building a bridge, no matter how essential to this movement. Whole quarters
of the United States, particularly in the new states,
and in the slave districts, are without roads necessary to a regular mail.   New Orleans, even with
invaluable productions, sometimes fails to get a
mail for weeks at a time, as we said, and its great
market all the time groping in the dark, and often
losing money by buying and selling at hazard.
This renders a people discontented, and sinks the
government into contempt with them, or in their
estimation.   They have, consequently, less patriotism and regard for the institutions of their country,
finding them thus unavailable, and liable to perverted constructions.   Can any thing but contempt attend on a power that cannot make a road,
must submit to chance the movements necessary
to a war, to the mails, to that intercourse so essential to comfort and unity, and to a varied and rich
commerce ? The people are taxed more to get
their supply of goods to the consuming points after
they reach our shores, than bringing them from
Europe or the Indies.   The mail, in order to get

along over such roads, has to charge two or three prices for a letter or newspaper. It costs more money to get a letter from Buffalo to New York, than it does a barrel of flour; more to get a letter from New York to New Orleans than a barrel of pork; because the sea is open for commerce, not for the mail, which has to take the mud. In the last war the commanding general at New Orleans was enforcing martial law, and imprisoning civil officers a month after peace was declared, because the mail could not bring the intelligence. It is indicative of a good government to find its communications perfect, its mail certain and rapid, and its tribunals of justice prompt and independent. Then the people feel together, act together, and have each other's sympathies and support.

The most alarming thing for all true patriots in regard to the post department is the deep and open corruption that runs through it. This wide-spread facility is seized by the corrupt and designing to operate upon and influence the great mass of ignorance that constitutes, in all countries, the large majority of the population. The party in power, through the mail, wields 20,000 franks in the deputy postmasters, and 1,000 others arising from the other departments and offices of the government, and can use them all for party purposes, because, having the appointment of all these, it can insure their subserviency. Tell me not that this will not be done. It has been done all the time within the last twelve years, is done now, and will be done so long as dishonesty rules the land. Could mathematics run through all this complexity of corruption and undue influence, I believe it might be proved that, within the time named, a certain party have maintained themselves in office, and insured the succession of their minions, more by the aids of these corruptions of the mail than all other circumstances put together. Into what part of the United States do we go, even the darkest corners thereof, without seeing the mail delivering whole stage loads of this party, one-sided, lying matter, in the shape of newspapers, letters, extras, and dictations of some kind, all franked, or to be franked, and distributed among the people? Whole packets are daily sent to deputy postmasters, who have their standing orders to put names on and distribute each number to some person in their neighborhood, ignorant enough to be influenced or vain enough to be flattered by this sort of attention. These officers are taxed a commission on their salaries, first, to frank these lying journals, and then their honesty taxed to give distribution to them. It never occurred to our Washingtons, Adamses, Madisons, Monroes, and such single-hearted honest men, that the 20,000 postmasters were to be converted into corrupt tools of party, as well as their offices; swear allegiance, act to dictation, and be taxed in their little salaries besides, to insure the continuance of their masters and themselves in power! Yet such has been the case. No honest man would believe the hundredth part of the facts, if truly stated, regarding the corruption of this department;

they exceed all previous conceptions, and would appal the honest citizens if made visible.

What is the remedy for this crying evil, this fully-fledged corruption? I answer, that all honest patriots who reflect on this subject say, that the nation is lost without a reform that reaches the very source of the corruption. The franking privilege, as useful as it might be made, must be discontinued, and denied not only to the 20,000 postmasters, but to our public officers, except the President. The tenures of the offices of the deputy postmasters must be made permanent, or during honest behavior, and placed beyond the power of not only the head of that department to remove, but the President himself; the interchanges of newspaper editors be prohibited or limited, and all useless matter that now goes free be either thrown out or made to pay. That all the matter that goes by mail be made to pay in advance, and all postage put down to the lowest possible rate that promises to pay. Nothing short of the above regulations will correct this hugest of all corruptions, or cleanse the Augean stable of political bribery and filth. Some writer has said, " Give me the making of the ballads, the people will sing, and I will govern them;" and I say, give me the mighty leverage of 20,000 active tools, with their 20,000 franks, and I will govern them with much more certainty. Honest newspapers or opposing journals, and frequently letters on business, are kept back, to make room for the mass of corruption that is claiming distribution for political effect. These 20,000 agents are placed in the very best positions for popular effect; and their own voices not only raised in favor of their dishonest employers, but backed by these innumerable, one-sided, lying letters and journals. Were all the matter thus availed of charged full postage, it would double the revenues of that department. Hence treble postage is charged on the honest citizen to enable the department to wield all this corruption, and obliges honest citizens to employ private mails, at one-third of the price, to insure to them certainty in the delivery and keep them out of this corrupt contact.

CHAPTER XXXI.

REPRESENTATION, PUBLIC OPINION, SUFFRAGE.

GOVERNMENTS are very much dependent upon public opinion, which is all-powerful when enlightened and free to act, with the facilities of rapid interchanges. It becomes, then, a capital object to render this opinion as intelligent as possible, and as prompt as any circumstances can render it. In Europe, now under monarchies, and many of them absolute, public opinion walks forth, and not only stays the hands of the rulers from violence and injustice, but directs their acts to the great purposes of the general good. The representation in Europe, constructed as it is, must be nominal, is very partial and defective, and, if it acted according to its constituent base, would be one-sided and unjust. Fortunately for those countries, an enlightened public opinion steps forward and supplies this glaring defect in the representation, and points so strongly and steadily to the real interests of those countries, that it must be obeyed, and does really control the minds of the rulers, and direct their policies and acts. All that this public opinion needs to render it efficient is to be intelligent, and for the citizens to hold rapid communications with one another, in every part of their own nations, and with other countries. England and France are proverbially under the influence of public opinion, which corrects the defects in a great degree of their representation. Prussia, and Austria, and the German States, although absolute in the construction of their governments, have become just and paternal by force of public opinion, and are now almost patterns of all that is just, wise, and efficient in governments. The high system of schools, and the broad principles of justice that are now a part of the very foundations of those countries, furnish some substitutes for a legislative representation and chambers. All the ameliorations nearly that the world is now making are from the impulses of public opinion. All interests become safe, and perfect guarantees spring up against any injustice or violence offered to persons and property, and repose mankind on this everlasting foundation. The English parliament and the French chambers are in their very basis so defective that, but for public opinion, the crown could control them and convert them into tools of power. They dare not do it, however, nor suborn them to act contrary to the general interest, fearful of this master of all, public opinion; which, identified with the general interests, steps forth and says to the monarch, " so far shalt thou go, and no farther," and has to be obeyed. Public opinion removed the Catholic disqualifications, and corrected the worst features of the rotten boroughs in England, and is now laboring to do away the oppression of the corn laws and the tithes, or so modify them as to make them less unjust. Public opinion is not confined in the old world to the civilized districts only; it is penetrating the barbarous and despotic regions of Russia, and is reaching the very palace of the Mussulman. The autocrat dares not disregard it, dares. not sport with the lives of his subjects, nor do flagrant or whimsical acts of injustice. The Grand Turk finds his account in some observance of justice, some amelioration of old forms, some relaxation of the intolerant pretensions so long acted upon.

I regard an enlightened public opinion as less liable to err, and a better safeguard for human rights and general interests, than a defective representation based on improper ratios, or constituted by that broad general suffrage that is under the influence of

party. A representation based on the rotten bor-
ough system, if it acts apart from public opinion,
is sure to be subsidized by the aristocracy ; and the
one based on a general suffrage that is brought up
to the polls by the designing, is sure to disregard the
better opinions of the citizens, and co-operate with
those who constitute it for selfish and corrupt purposes. This last sort of representation is harder
to control than any other, because it feels secure on
this broad basis of general suffrage, and, wielding
it, puts at defiance legitimate public opinion, and
boldly delights in injustice and selfishness. Instead
of the ignorant, the unsubstantial, and the foreigners, without any hold on the country or interest in
it, that our demagogues and designing politicians
now marshal at the polls, there should be voters
who, from their own impulses of patriotism and
substantial interest, would sustain the great policies
of the nation. How are these to be insured and
made to prevail ? I answer, in no other way than
by confining the suffrage to the intelligent and
substantial of the nation. Experience now tells
us, in a language too plain to be mistaken, that the
suffrages of any nation must rest upon a property
qualification, in order to insure prosperity and national honor. Such voters would send forth the
proper sort of representatives, and support those
policies and enactments calculated to advance the
country—not party designs. Party spirit then would
be hushed, unworthy and dishonest motives banished our legislative halls, and views of high na-

tional interest all the time uppermost. The struggle for the loaves and fishes, the odious and corrupt
doctrine that "to the victors belong the spoils,"
would be scouted from our councils and cabinets,
and give place to a pure patriotism that would
breathe forth its aspirations for the public good.
I would feel that all was safe, if I could see an enlightened public opinion lifted above the broad and
corrupt basis of a general suffrage, and taking the
direction of affairs. It would then speak as loudly
at the polls as in the legislatures and councils, and
bear its corrective in a way to be available.

How is public opinion to be enlightened enough
in this country to be an efficient guide and corrective? We have, as said before, been all the time
spreading our thin texture to the far west, until we
have no tenacity, no sympathies in common, no
efficient education. Our national government, we
have seen, has eschewed all interference or control
of education, and left it to chance or the states;
and no system can reach our people, scattered as
they are in the wilds, and instruct them. The very
mails fail to find them in a way regular enough to
impart to them the proper information, in the prompt
way necessary to connect their movements with the
business operations of the day. People are as much
or more enlightened by rapid interchanges of
thought, and the action of their sympathies upon
each other, as by any system of education.

CHAPTER XXXII.

STATE DEBTS, CITY DEFENCES, AND LICENSES TO SELL
SPIRITS.

WE are now in a condition of great distress and
even discredit from our state debts. The policy that
incurred them, through impolitic and much to be de-
precated, is not the question now ; they exist, and
how to get rid of them becomes the all-absorbing
topic for our politicians. In nearly half of the
cases, the expenditures have accomplished no good
purpose, and the debts too large to be wielded by
the states that incurred them ; hence the interest
on nearly half lies unprovided for, and in some cases
the debts themselves have been repudiated, greatly
to the disgrace of the country. Although the constitution prohibits the states issuing bills of credit,
(and what can be a stronger bill of credit than a
state bond or state stock ?) yet the debts are incurred, and the disgrace, like the darts that all the
beasts in the Zodiac point to the good man in the
front page of almanacs, impales our federal government and wounds its tenderest parts. The capitalists abroad look upon us as one government, and
are not expected to make the distinction between

state sovereignties and our general government; scarcely do the nations of Europe, much less the individual creditors, make such a distinction. An obligation seems to rest on our federal government, from the necessity of the case, to step forward and wipe off these unconstitutional and foul tracks of the local sovereignties, and redeem the nation from the disgrace. Not only the character of any good and proper government wants to be vindicated from all such reproaches, but more especially these United States, who are held as a sort of sample government, a sort of last test of the great principles of republicanism. If a charge of unfairness and shuffling should be fastened upon us, as is likely to be the case, it will not only injure us, but the great cause of free government in which we have embarked, and give occasion for the enemies of human rights to triumph. The precedents that England, France, and the United States, have established towards Mexico and the South American republics, that of making the government responsible for the debts, defalcations, and even spoliations of the subject, and recognized in the Beaumarchais case that entered into our arrangement with France, go to show the right and the inclination both, of the governments to which the creditors appertain, to interfere in the case, and make it the subject of a negotiation, and even war if necessary. Our state debts may on that principle cost us a war, and that would create a debt of twice their amount. Our federal government certainly finds itself in a very unpleasant and dishonorable dilemma on this subject. When asked to assume these debts she answers, that they are state debts, that those states are sovereign and beyond her control, and that she has nothing to do with it. The foreign government then travels down to the indebted state and undertakes to force it to pay, when, as soon as any preparations are made to oblige her to pay, the federal government interferes, espouses her cause, and protects from reprisal the indebted state. This looks very much like collusion, and proves how hollow and fraudulent in its results the declaration that she had nothing to do with it really was. This sort of juggling will not satisfy the world, nor vindicate the character of our government from fraud and dishonor, for there really seems to be both in the case.

The revenues of this government are now teeming, and promise an overflowing treasury for years to come. This shows an ability, and places the case upon grounds without any excuse. Two hundred millions of stock issued by the federal government, bearing an interest of three and a half per cent., would take up all these disgraceful debts, which, making only seven millions a year of interest, would not be felt, and would not even absorb our surplus revenue. Our politicians ought to wake up to this disgrace, and labor to overcome the action of that party that does not feel the dishonor or the necessity of having a government free from reproach or charges of fraud, and a want of high and

honorable sentiments.   For the character of republics this should be done, as well as to aid the great
cause of liberty ; like Cæsar's wife, they should
not only be pure, but unsuspected.

City defences.   Another subject has arisen since
our cities have grown so much, and are filled with
reckless foreigners and mobs, as to the best and
most effectual remedy for the growing disorders
and violences that prevail in them. The substance
and all the interests both of persons and property
are threatened by the lawless, the idle and vicious
So far all the police established in our cities seems
to fail on the great occasions of mobs and riots
The Mayor and his staff, backed by a meagre con-
stabulary, become powerless, and are pushed aside
and disregarded in such affrays.   Let us first inquire into the root of the evil, and then discuss
some remedy for it.   The primary cause of the
whole disorder is found in the general suffrage that
prevails in the city elections.   All vote that are
found in the city, or have been a few months there,
without any interest or hold on the community.
The vagabonds, the loafers, the paupers, and desperate strangers brought over and turned loose upon
the town, are all voters, and are embodied and
brought up to the polls by the designing and office
seekers ; and by the aid of such votes not only put
in office, but supported in their ultra measures
against the property of the citizens, and in favor of
this class of voters.   They dare not do their duty
when it bears upon vice and idleness, because they

are dependent upon them for their office, and must compromise with all disorder for the same reasons. This unprincipled and mutual support between the office-holders and voters is the cause of all the disorder, arrests every attempt to correct it, and laughs at the ultimate tendency of the thing and the disgrace incident thereto. In our cities all the guarantees for the safety of persons and property seem to be lost, and a sad foreboding for the future nestles gloomily in the hearts of all property-holders and good citizens.

Some hope has been lit up lately from the action of the organized militia companies that exist in our cities, and a vain belief entertained that they would be adequate to the purposes of good order. This idea is fallacious, because most of those companies have a fellow feeling with the mob, as was manifest in Philadelphia; and where, if they do act, so much odium and bitterness attend it, that the militia are run down, their persons and properties endangered, both secretly and publicly; and instead of getting the thanks of the community, and being regarded as patriots, are rendered so unpopular that they have to abandon their organization. Most of the individuals in those companies belonging to the lower classes have quit them from fellow feeling with the mob; another portion, through fear of their popularity, and future prospects of ambition; which leaves only a few large property-holders, altogether inadequate to the purposes of defence against such odds. Another hope rested upon the idea that cities would come to the necessity of employing a standing army or police strong enough to keep order. This, too, is fallacious, because the persons who generally compose mobs have a majority of voters, and will take care to put in such officers as will not take any such strong measures against them; for as well might you expect the vicious and reckless to punish themselves directly, as to do it indirectly, through the officers that they create and control. The only remedy, then, is in correcting the elective franchise, and taking away the right of suffrage from the unsubstantial and unsettled. Let the substance take care of itself at the polls, and the good order and justice that appertain to men of substance and such as are permanently settled, will be a guarantee for the safety of persons, and insure the proper administration of justice. The mayor and councils should hold their offices longer, be more independent, and have the power to inquire into the means of living of every individual in the corporation. They should compel every individual to account for his or her mode of living and movements, and to allow none to remain in idleness and vice. The case is one of crying necessity, and unless a change be put in train, all the property in our cities will become jeopardized, all persons unsafe, capital and investments avoid them, and all business be affected in them. No hope arises from the national government, that has no troops to spare, and so many state-right and constitutional questions to be settled before it acts, that it would be too late to prevent destruction.

Licenses to sell spirits. In these days of temperance and the good cause that is trying to save mankind from their own follies and bad habits, all aids should be given to them by our laws and authorities. We have now light and experience enough to decide, without any sort of question, against allowing or licensing the sale of spirituous liquors in any retail way. There is no question in the minds of the thinking part of the community, but that all our disorders and outbreaking vices are the results of drink and drunkenness. Since then the majority of the worth and the best interests of the country are pointing to and denouncing this habit as most ruinous to the morals and property of the country, why not stop, by legislative enactments its open and overwhelming course ? What stays the hands of our state legislatures, and the heads of our corporations, from putting an immediate stop to it by withholding all licenses to retail spirituous liquors ? The general suffrage here speaks also, and having the votes, forbids our legislators and officers from acting as the interests of the country require, because so many worthless voters are in the habit of drinking, that they by their clamor, zeal, and numbers, deter those dependent upon such votes from all attempts at a prohibition of the evil. Most of the disorders that are fastened upon the country, as well as all the evils threatened, depend for their support on this principle. Our public opinion, then, cannot be very influential or prompt in controlling either the elections or legislative enactments thus scattered, thus ignorant, and thus defeated by an unworthy suffrage. We were met at the very entrance into national existence by this scattering condition, by a want of education and sympathy among the people, and this utter prostitution of the sacred elective franchise, which prevented all unity of action, and all singleness of purpose, and implanted the seeds of political corruption in our very bosoms. Suffrage conceded is gone forever, because it can only be called back by the ballot boxes or a revolution; the former, being the majority, will not vote a disfranchisement of themselves, and revolutions wipe out with blood and despotism in such a case.

A perfect representation requires to be based on just ratios of population, and the substance of the land. Without both of these elements it is liable to be controlled either by the aristocracy or the corruption of demagogues. Public opinion, however enlightened, weighs naught with the rabble of a general suffrage, which glories in bearing down all before it of worth or excellence. A representation rightly constructed is the best, perhaps the only guarantee, for the safety of persons and property, and constitutes the very foundation of all safe and free government. This is the true palladium of liberty, guards from defilement her sacred shrines, and stands man forth the free and noble being the God of nature intended him to be;

claiming to govern himself. Constitutions go for nothing under the angry or interested passions of men; charters are a mockery without this support, and the concessions of the rulers of mankind as frail as their breath that granted them. A representation based on the worth, the intelligence and substance of the land, stands forward the friend of human rights, superior to aristocracy, above the gusts of party feeling, and true to the firm foundation upon which it rests. It cannot become corrupt, for its source is too pure, and if it errs, a recurrence to the same pure source, the ballot boxes, corrects all its aberrations, and keeps it identified with the people. Our representation has sundry defects too deeply seated to be corrected, because coeval with the government, and stamped in its very origin upon it by the sovereignties of these states : I mean that construction of the Senate, which gives to the small old states and the weak and crude new ones equal power with the rich and populous ones, and the clause which allows three-fifths of the slaves to vote. These two provisions interfere with all just ratios, and all first principles of justice and right, but are a part of us, and must remain, because the peace and harmony of the confederation require it. With such defects our representation calls still louder for an enlightened public opinion to counteract and control them, and prevent any undue use being made of them. If our representation, besides bearing in its bosom these constitutional defects, be corrupted in its very source by this general suffrage, and perverted into base, grovelling, and interested channels, instead of its being this guarantee of safety, this palladium of liberty we speak of, it then subserves party purposes, and becomes a pretext and cover under which the designing sap all resources, destroy all rational liberty, and degrade all our institutions, until the nation, without character or honor, or any available policy, sinks into contempt. In all countries where a general suffrage rakes up and embraces the worthless, the unsubstantial, and the ignorant, a set of designing politicians never fail to control them, and bring them up to the polls to carry all the elections, and through them secure to themselves the influence in the legislatures. A feeling is soon lit up in this class against all the wealth, intelligence, and refinement in the country, which they are taught to brand as aristocrats and proud, and a total separation takes place very much to the injury of both. The patronage extended to, and the influence exerted upon, the ignorant lower classes, by the wealthy, refined, and well-mannered, would be greatly beneficial if nothing stood in the way, would soften their manners, inform their minds, and render them every way better citizens and more happy. All that is lost by letting them in to the polls, as well as the best policies of the nation; and instead thereof a morose feeling, a secret hatred, and an unrelenting war waged upon the worth and even property of the nation. Agrarian views, political corruption, the success of demagogues, and the loss of all true patriotism and national honor follow in the train, until all is lost, abused, or perverted. Give us a proper suffrage, a sound representation, and an enlightened public opinion, and all will not only be safe but prosperous and happy.

CHAPTER XXXIII.

NEW STAPLES, SILK, INDIGO, GRAPE, OLIVE, MORE SUGAR AND WOOL, MADDER AND WOAD, ETC., AND AMELIORATIONS IN AGRICULTURE.

We have spoken of agriculture and its productions in a general way, and how they would be affected by a tariff. We will here show how it can be extended, ameliorated, and ornamented. Political economy ought never to lose sight of this real basis of the world's prosperity and support. The proper discriminations should be made of the different sorts of staples and things within the capacity of a country to grow, and encourage by protection or bounties such as tend to enrich the country and vary its productions the most. Small inducements often would introduce a new and valuable culture, when there is spare labor, and a soil and climate suitable for it, and it would not interfere with other cultures. Variety in agriculture should be aimed at, as apt to hit the markets, and is nearly as important in this department as in manufactures. In such a varied product there are more chances for a profit, nationally speaking, and more certainty of some available export. We have already much variety and richness in our agricultural productions, as well as great volume, brought about by individual exertions which count us largely. We will now undertake to show what other cultures we might introduce with great advantage, and to the relief of others that are overcharged. I have already alluded to the silk culture, and proved that it is admirably adapted to most of the United States, and calculated to bring into value and productiveness the labor of women and children without abstracting them from their dear homes, and that it will leave all the strong male labor for the out-door operations on the farm. A little bounty or a high protecting tariff would do this much sooner, and in a very few years give us one of the most valuable and elegant staples in the world. The product might be made to amount, in a year or two, to twenty million pounds of silk, worth forty to fifty million dollars to the country. Two acres, as we have said, are enough to grow the trees upon to feed worms enough to produce fifty pounds of raw silk, and six weeks the time required to feed the worms. Five hundred thousand families engaged in the United States growing silk, at fifty pounds to each family, amounts to twenty-five million pounds of silk, which is more than England and all the North of Europe want.

We want also many articles necessary to our manufactories, such as indigo, madder, and woad, all of which grow well in our country, and for all which we have a plenty of spare labor. We require more wool too, and of a greater variety, suitable for blankets, stuff goods, and fine shawls, as well as clothes. To arrive at this variety, a tariff should encourage it enough to warrant the importation of all the sorts of sheep and goats, and the Peruvian animals. We do not make sugar enough for our own consumption by more than one half, and should encourage labor into that production. We have soil and climate enough to produce up to the home market, if rightly encouraged, and thereby much relieve the cotton which is so much overdone. We consume largely of fruits, wine, and oils, and have large districts of poor sandy or rocky territory fitted for nothing else, that would admirably suit those cultures, and thus render them of some avail. Let us now see what we might save annually by cultivating these things—say in silk ten million dollars, in wool four millions, in sugar four millions, in wines four millions, in fruit and oil two millions, in dye-stuffs one million, all of which would amount to twenty-five million dollars made annually, or saved, which is the same thing. This vast saving too would not be at the expense of any other production, but greatly to the relief of all, as all are overdone, and could well spare labor.

Under the idea of ameliorations in agriculture, we would encourage, by protection and bounties, the importation of all fine and useful animals, from which to breed and improve our stock; for a fine animal eats no more, hardly as much, as a bad one. Sample farms should be got up in every part of the United States, under the protection of the federal or state government, and made the depositories of all improvements, in such a way that all might see by inspection the benefits of any new or useful invention. A good system of manuring becomes of national concern, and should be aided by the encouragement of the importation of guano, lime, gypsum, bones, poudrette, and all such highly available stimulants and aids in the productions of the soil, and rewards offered for the discovery or compounding of these things at home. A proper system of manures would arrest that process of exhaustion that is going on annually to an alarming extent in the southern portions of the United States, and enable the country to put on a cheerful, improving appearance, instead of the blank exhaustion, gullies, and dilapidation, that now shock the mind of the true patriot. Another good effect would flow from a system of manuring that would arrest exhaustion: that of preventing our people emigrating so widely, and scattering themselves so inefficiently in the west, and thereby losing all the advantages to society and improvements attendant on more dense settlements. Much may be done for the good health and productiveness of a country, to have it well drained by the proper ditches, and secured by proper embankments from the inundations of the rivers. This is often too great an undertaking for individuals, as long lines of ditches and embankments extending through several districts are to be constructed, and rivers straightened. Such things should be done by the proper engineers, under laws of the government, or charters granted to the proper persons. Draining a country not only renders it more healthy, which is all important, but prevents too much moisture, and those swarms of insects that destroy all our fruit and annoy our persons so much.

Our climate is subject to such great extremes of heat and cold, and sudden in its transitions from the one to the other, that it becomes very trying on the health and constitutions of our people. The government should look to that, and provide for a suitable clothing to meet these extremes. A warm, cheap, woollen covering is all important to our laborers that are exposed, such as flannels, blankets, bear-skin, swansdown, or fearnought cloths, which should be established beyond all necessity of looking abroad for these things. Since our laborers began to use more flannel in their clothing and next to their skins, they are more healthy This indispensable article is still too dear, as well as all the others that we have named, and should be protected enough to insure their being made in the country, and as cheap as possible from our own competition. Our people then would not suffer so much

from consumptions, inflammatory attacks, and ca-
tarrhs. Encouragement should also be given by
premiums, and so forth, to induce warmer houses to
be built. Stone or brick would be much warmer
than the thin, wooden shells that we now build,
within which we are chilled into colds and ill
health every winter. The New England popular
tion do not show their usual shrewdness in this respect, in removing the material nature gave to them,
fine stone, from the very foundations where they
set their shells of wood houses. This wood, too,
often costs money, and requires to be brought from
a great distance; whereas the stone occupies the
ground, and is in the way of this factitious building which they resort to.

There are some cultures that in their nature
scarcely ever fail, and for that reason are available
to all wise and regular governments. I will instance the Irish potato crop in Europe. Before
this culture became common in the English dominions in Europe, they leaned mainly upon the wheat
crop for their support. Any thing happening to
this single crop, the whole population suffered, and
the poor intensely, from the rise that would take
place at such times. With the wheat crop there
was but a single chance, and if a very wet or very
dry season prevailed, or insects, or rust, this crop
was so affected that it became jeopardized; and
the poor, with all the precaution of opening the
ports to grain, would frequently suffer much and
long. The nation was often impoverished and its

specie drawn away to buy corn to save its people from starving. The potato was introduced, changed the whole face of the thing, and saved the nation from scarcely any future suffering; for this being a certain crop, not affected by moisture, or rust, or insects—the great enemies of the wheat—was always ready with its cheap and abundant supply of a good substitute for bread, to relieve the great mass of the people. The best writers now admit that in England, Ireland, and Scotland, the potato relieves from the consumption of wheat bread three-fourths of the whole population each and every year; and when the wheat crop fails, seven-eighths of the population consume potatoes. No scarcity then can produce much, if any, suffering, because the better classes then need only lean the heavier upon the potato crop. Two chances are thus given in the year for food : the one a winter or spring crop—wheat, barley, rye, and oats; and the other, a fall crop of the potatoes. The one or the other is sure to hit, and often both. Nothing has gone so far to keep down into quiet and good order the whole population of the north of Europe, as the potato culture. When a people are mad, or rather infuriated, with hunger, they stop at nothing, but break down all before them. Bayonets and muskets, or even cannon, offer no terrors to the starving; they rush into all and every danger after food, and not only despoil those who hoard it, but war upon all wealth and plenty. The good order then of society, the morals of a people, the very safety and existence of a government, depend upon the certainty of food, if not upon its quality. Political economy ought to hail this culture, this good, and wholesome, and palatable, and order-producing vegetable, as a blessing to the human family, and one of the surest supports of a good government. Could the introducer of the potato culture be known, all mankind should rush forth and erect a monument to him, as one of the very best and greatest benefactors to man.

We in this country have, all the time, two chances for a crop: the Indian corn, buckwheat, and potatoes, are summer and fall crops, along with the thousands of vegetables that then flourish; and the wheat, rye, oats, and barley, which are winter or spring crops;—between the two chances we have hardly ever a scarcity of magnitude enough to lead to suffering. The supply of food has been all the time a very certain thing in this country, and none of our disorders or irregularities are owing to that cause. Our politicians ought to encourage this diversity of chances and of crops all the time, and if individual inclination be not enough, other inducements ought to be offered. Our agricultural societies, too, should urge the thing in every possible way, and write articles in the journals, giving reasons for it, and offering premiums, if any one should drop behind and need it.

FINIS.